AF428698

The Degrees of Wellness
Six Rules to Creating a Healthy Union Through Self-Discovery and Personal Growth

Christine A. Benjamin

Dedication

To My Beloved Family,

This book is dedicated to you, my precious sons, and the remarkable woman who has been a guiding light in my life, my mother. You are the ones who have inspired me to embark on this journey of exploring the six degrees of wellness and sharing my insights with the world.

To my boys, you are my pride and joy. Your boundless curiosity, unwavering love, and playful spirits have filled my life with immeasurable happiness. As I delve into the intricacies of wellness, I am reminded of the importance of nurturing your physical, mental, emotional, and spiritual well-being. May this book serve as a compass to guide you on your wellness journey as you embark on your journey as a man.

To my dear mother, you are my rock and pillar of strength. Your unwavering support, wisdom, and unconditional love have shaped me into who I am today. As I explore the six dimensions of wellness in this book, I am grateful for the valuable lessons you have taught me about the interconnectedness of our well-being. Your constant presence in my life has been a beacon of inspiration, and I am honored to dedicate this book to you.

To my wise grandmother in heaven, I continue to heed your guiding words and feel your loving spirit. Thank you for being my best friend in my most trying times.

Thank you, family, for being my motivation and my driving force. Your presence in my life has enriched it beyond measure, and I am forever grateful for the love and support you provide. May this book be a testament to the profound impact you have had on my life and the profound bond we share.

With all my love,

Christine

Acknowledgment

I would like to express my gratitude to Source, God, my Angelic Team for providing me with the inspiration and guidance to write this book on the six dimensions of wellness.

My dear friend, Aaron "Sahpreem" King, you've inspired and encouraged me to write this book for many years, and I'm amazed at the journey it took to get here. Your dedication to being a sounding board, cheerleader, guide, and friend has truly shown me the value of having people like you in my life, and I can assure you there are not many. Thank you for your valued friendship and guidance over the decades, and cheers to continued growth within ourselves and our propelled vision to change the world.

I also want to thank my family and friends for their unwavering support throughout this journey as well as my production team for all of their hard work and dedication to this project. Finally, I would like to acknowledge all those who have contributed to my spiritual growth and development over the years.

About the Author

No one is a perfect person. But why not strive to be the version of us that comes closest to perfection?

Christine Antionette Benjamin was born and raised in Jamaica, Queens, NY. Growing up in the '70s and '80s, she was heavily influenced by music, the arts, and her community. She grew up in an era where going outside and gathering her crew of friends to play handball in the park was normal and happened quite often.

Even at that age, she spent most of her time in the company of her friends and learned much about human behaviors and actions. Those days were key parts of the story of her growth and understanding of her role in society. Christine's thought process and challenging the 'normal' has always pushed her to consider beyond what is seen and commonly understood; because *normal* is not always what's best.

Christine believes that sometimes, our lives are carbon copies of our parents' and grandparents' lives—although, they are not always in alignment with our own personal soul's journey.

She is fascinated with uncovering people's true value and showing them how to live a fulfilling and harmonious life. Over the course of several decades, she has developed the tools to help herself and her community. She has many years of esoteric study and acquiring knowledge of divination tools to assist her and her clients on her belt.

She believes tools such as numerology, astrology, human design, destiny cards, reiki, and tarot, connect our higher self and spiritual teams that help guide us through life. She has also studied emotional intelligence, physical communication, and the human psyche. She relies heavily upon her intuition when consulting clients to tune into their core soul desires. She then helps them to uncover the shadow aspects of their lives.

She does this so they may realize their hidden potential and grow into a better version of themselves. Over several years of training and teaching, Christine has come to realize that the six aspects reviewed in this book are areas that are usually most distorted and hinder people from forming healthy bonds and boundaries.

With this book, she hopes to share information that will be a catalyst for change for some and an achievement checklist for others.

Preface

The Eight Dimensions of Wellness

Wellness is such a broad concept. Our cultural perspectives and life experiences have an impact on how we view it. We can define wellness as the state of one being aware, self-directed, holistically developing, multifaceted, affirming, and inclusive. For us to genuinely grow, we must pay attention to all facets of our well-being.

All dimensions don't have to be in perfect equilibrium. Finding personal harmony with the aspects that resonate with you or are most true to you is the objective instead. Passively getting there is not an option; you must be conscious, actively accepting, and committed.

Physical Wellness

When we think of 'health,' we generally focus on our physical condition first. However, physical wellness is more than just being free of sickness, which is how we often define it. Physical wellness is all about taking care of your body so that you may live a long, healthy, and active life. This aspect of our well-being necessitates developing healthy behaviors and maintaining them throughout time. For our bodies to work properly and feel well, we need to eat a balanced diet and engage in frequent fitness-activities while avoiding dangerous circumstances and substances, including alcohol, smoking, and narcotics. Pay attention to your body, attend all of your doctor's visits and vaccinations, and get enough rest. You only have one body, so make it your top priority!

Emotional Wellness

Developing an awareness and acceptance of your feelings, actions, beliefs, and attitudes is a key component of emotional well-being. It also entails exploring and controlling your emotions and respecting others' sentiments. It takes work to become emotionally aware, yet developing this ability can help us take control and recover from challenges in life.

Our emotional wellness and general hardiness may be improved by regularly practicing self-care, setting reasonable expectations, adopting constructive and healthy coping mechanisms, and cultivating relationships with others.

It's important to note that the terms *"emotional well-being"* and *"mental wellness"* can be used interchangeably, but they are not the same thing. One aspect of mental well-being is focused on how well your mind processes events and information. The way those ideas and feelings are communicated is related to emotional well-being.

It's crucial to get assistance whenever necessary to maintain a good attitude while you attempt to improve your well-being since the relationship between mental and emotional health can be complicated.

Social Wellness

Making a good impact on society, engaging with your community, and developing healthy connections with others are all aspects of social well-being. Being conscious of your tastes and background is the first step in achieving this aspect of well-being. For instance, it's possible that you like a different kind, volume, or frequency of sociability than others do.

We must appreciate variety, be receptive to the social and cultural backgrounds of others, and be sensitive to be socially healthy. This means that we need to be aware of and accepting of diversity.

True social well-being requires developing and maintaining a secure, encouraging, welcoming, and pleasant interpersonal and group interactions. Feelings of belonging and social welfare may be influenced by taking pleasure in social interaction, making enduring friendships, and maintaining good interpersonal relationships.

Financial Wellness

Being financially healthy requires being careful with your money and resource management. Budgeting and learning to live within your means are essential components of financial wellness. You may satisfy your short- and long-term demands, fulfill financial commitments, and accomplish reasonable financial objectives with sound money management techniques.

Making wise investment choices and having an emergency plan are two other financial issues. Well-handled finances lessen stress and concern by providing a greater feeling of stability and security.

Think about what kind of connection you have with money!

The values, beliefs, upbringing, culture, and a host of other characteristics that a person possesses may all impact how they feel about money. Remember that everyone has different financial demands and situations. Financial wellness is more about developing valuable skills and taking action that fits your goals than it is about having money.

Spiritual Wellness

Spiritual well-being may be characterized as looking for motivation, contemplating the meaning of life, or leading a purposeful, intentional existence.

This is a highly private endeavor that is based on a person's values and beliefs. It might or might not involve worship, religious observance, the notion of a higher power, sacrosanct rites, or cultural customs. Some people achieve serenity via mindfulness, yoga, or meditation. Others discover harmony by getting in touch with nature.

Others discover spiritual well-being through introspection, self-examination, thankfulness, or leading a charitable and compassionate life. Having a strong sense of right and wrong helps us make decisions and directs our behavior. Working on the spiritual side of wellness strengthens our inner tenacity and enables us to live gracefully.

Intellectual Wellness

Intellectual wellness refers to the state of being actively engaged in learning, growing, and expanding your knowledge and skills. This dimension of wellness is important because it helps keep the mind active and engaged, which can positively impact overall health and well-being.

Intellectual wellness involves continuously challenging the mind, learning new things, and seeking new experiences. This can be achieved through activities such as reading, attending educational events, engaging in hobbies, or pursuing a new skill. In addition, intellectual wellness also involves being open to new ideas, seeking diverse perspectives, and having an inquisitive and curious mind.

Having intellectual wellness can bring a sense of purpose, fulfillment, and meaning to life. It can also enhance decision-making skills and problem-solving abilities, improving personal and professional success. Encouraging and pursuing intellectual wellness can lead to a more dynamic and well-rounded life and a more adaptable mind that can better handle life's challenges.

Occupational Wellness

Occupational wellness refers to the balance and satisfaction between one's work and other aspects of life. It involves finding meaning, purpose, and fulfillment in one's work and making it a positive aspect of one's overall well-being.

Occupational wellness means having a job that provides a sense of purpose, challenge, and satisfaction. It also means balancing work demands with other aspects of life, such as relationships, hobbies, and self-care. This can be achieved by setting realistic expectations, managing time effectively, and engaging in activities outside of work that bring joy and balance to life. Occupational wellness also involves seeking and finding work that aligns with one's values, skills, and interests. This can lead to a greater sense of purpose, fulfillment, and satisfaction in work. Additionally, having occupational wellness can lead to improved financial stability, which can positively impact other dimensions of wellness, such as financial and emotional wellness.

It's important to continuously reflect on and assess one's occupational wellness and make changes as necessary to achieve a fulfilling and balanced work-life.

Environmental Wellness

Environmental wellness refers to the relationship between an individual and their surrounding environment. It involves understanding and appreciating the environmental impact of our actions and seeking to live in harmony with the natural world.

Having environmental wellness means being aware of and sensitive to environmental issues and making an effort to reduce one's carbon footprint. This can be achieved by reducing waste, conserving resources, using environmentally friendly products, and engaging in activities that promote environmental health, such as recycling and gardening.

Environmental wellness also involves connecting with and appreciating nature. This can be achieved through activities such as hiking, camping, or simply spending time outdoors in nature. This connection with the natural world can bring a sense of peace, balance, and rejuvenation to one's life.

Environmental wellness can also positively impact other dimensions of wellness, such as physical, emotional, and spiritual wellness. By understanding and appreciating our relationship with the environment, we can live more sustainably and in harmony with the world around us, promoting overall well-being.

These are the eight dimensions of wellness. Throughout this book, I intend to use these to further develop the ideas discussed in the six parts of the book. In doing so, I intend to show how one can live a happy life and have a fulfilling relationship!

Foreword

Life is a vast, multifaceted journey. To navigate it truly, one must grasp the concept of holistic Wellness, which extends beyond the conventional four directions. Imagine a compass that does not merely point north, south, east, or west but towards eight definitive dimensions, each beckoning us toward a richer understanding of well-being.

In "The Degrees of Wellness: Six Rules to Creating a Healthy Union Through Self-Discovery and Personal Growth," Christine Benjamin explores this intricate tapestry. She draws us into a world where Physical Wellness isn't just about health but is the vessel of our life's voyage. Emotional Wellness, far from being just feelings, is a deep dive into our very souls. With Social Wellness, we learn to bond and blend with our surrounding world, and Financial Wellness becomes the backbone to chasing and achieving dreams.

Christine's wisdom delves deeper, offering insights into Spiritual Wellness as our tether to the greater mysteries of existence. Intellectual Wellness reignites the ever-curious child in us, Occupational Wellness redefines professional satisfaction, and Environmental Wellness ties us back to the world, encouraging a harmonious coexistence with nature.

Having had the privilege of Christine's friendship for nearly twenty years, I've been a direct beneficiary of her deep insights and wisdom. Our countless conversations, laden with lessons about life and its myriad facets, have consistently pointed towards one truth: Wellness is a continuous journey of self-discovery.

The essence of Christine can be captured in one word: "connected." She's attuned not just to the world's palpable rhythm but to its unseen harmonies as well.

This connection has been a beacon for many, including myself, showing us paths paved with love, hope, and a profound understanding of life's intricacies.

Her book embodies this very spirit. When Christine shared her intention to encapsulate her insights into written form, I pondered how such vast wisdom could be confined to pages.

Yet, here we are—with a guide that is as profound as it is transformative.

I invite you to immerse yourself in this journey. As you explore each dimension, may you unearth your unique balance, resonate with the wisdom, and find a renewed purpose, joy, and fulfillment in life.

By the journey's end, I assure you, you'll emerge with a deeper, richer perspective on Wellness and well-being.

Aaron "Sahpreem" King

Spiritual Alchemist, Founder of Soular Astronauts™

Contents

PART I
1st Dimension: Emotional Wellness

CHAPTER.1

Toxic Traits

"Growth is painful. Change is painful. But, nothing is as painful as staying stuck where you do not belong."

-NR Narayana Murthy

Change is a necessary part of life. Yet, the process of changing is the hardest thing to accomplish. You have to step out of your comfort zone and enter a world that is, in many ways, unknown to you. As humans, the desire to evolve and change is built into our genes. We are made to adapt to changing conditions and environments around us. It happens so slowly that we are oblivious to this change until it has happened. But then again, there are people who are opposed to change. The two main reasons why we are not able to accept change is that we are comfortable with our old way of life and we are fearful of losing control.

We feel uncomfortable changing our old ways because;

- Everything seems different; we have to learn it all over again

- More work than before

- Change can hurt us financially or emotionally

Additionally, the second reason is the fear of losing control because change comes from letting go of old habits and embracing new ones. Most people are scared of this aspect because of the following reasons:

- Loss of control – You might temporarily lose control due to uncertainty and lack of knowledge of what the changes bring.

- Loss of face – Since we're social creatures, we tend to pay more attention to our social standing in society.

- Ripple effect – Changing one thing can potentially lead to a change in other areas of your life that could ultimately lead to you changing your daily life.

- Fear of incompetence. Not everyone is comfortable looking like they don't know what they're doing. Change can sometimes be disarming as it pushes one into foreign territory that is often out of our comfort zone.

If you aren't prepared to tackle these things, they can take over your life and hold you down. All these can make you reluctant to change your current ways and move toward a new future. Change doesn't always happen on a personal level. It can also occur around us. It can be in the shape of a new app, device, or technology; if it provides a new and different way of doing things, people will find it difficult to change their ways.

Change and You

Human beings are creatures of habit. When conditioned to doing something over time, we become so used to it that we do not want to let go, even if something is toxic for us. Even if we understand that the situation we are in is detrimental to our mental health and well-being, we remain trapped in that cycle because of how we are wired.

Evolutionary psychology explains that when our safe space is threatened, we tend to fight back. For us to even take the initiative to modify our routine is extremely demanding, to the point that it almost seems impossible. Most of us tend to shy away from such things, even if they are minute ones. However, we do not realize that change is imperative to personal growth.

When we remain stuck in the same place, it affects us in ways we do not even realize. It incapacitates us because we don't evolve in the way we should. As a result, our growth becomes stagnant, and we reach the point where we just stop realizing things. To be able to develop as a person, it is crucial that we focus on change and realize that it is a constant in life. Our journey to becoming the best versions of ourselves is a very long one, but we can only work through it when we realize the importance of letting go of traits that are detrimental to our being. The sooner we understand this, the sooner we can begin our journey of adapting to change, no matter how difficult it seems. Being likable as human beings is important to ensure healthy relationships with others around us, be it friends, family, or significant others. Therefore, we need to exude a positive and friendly vibe to attract people.

For that, we need to understand what our toxic traits are and then let go of them slowly and steadily by embracing change in small parts. This brings us to the understanding of a fundamental concept: emotional stability.

Emotional Stability

Emotional stability is one of the five big personality traits that we have. It refers to the ability of a person to remain calm and stable in a given situation. An emotionally stable person has good control over their emotions. Therefore, emotional stability is considered a desirable trait for human beings.

Emotional Stability vs. Emotional Instability

Emotionally stable people can easily withstand challenging situations without panicking and stressing too much. On the other hand, someone who is not emotionally stable would be considered irrational or be known for taking abrupt and sudden decisions in a moment's frenzy.

Dr. Ashley B Hampton describes emotional instability as, *"Emotional instability usually means some unpredictability in emotions and reactions to events."*

For example, you can;

- Lash out at others in the most unexpected way because they said something.

- Be easily frustrated from minor inconveniences, for example, unconsciously honking while stuck in traffic.

- Constantly shift moods; this can result from not having control over your emotions, usually anger.

These are all examples of situations where we tend to react in ways that we least expect ourselves to, not realizing that this is a toxic trait. A rare occurrence of such behavior is natural. However, frequent outbursts could mean that a person is emotionally unstable.

To have healthy relationships, we need to understand the importance of emotional stability and make conscious efforts to control our emotions in situations where it is most needed. It is absolutely normal to lose control once in a while, but when it becomes a habit, it affects us in ways than one. Compromised relationships are the result of that. When we become unpleasant, others naturally tend to stay away from us.

We tend to repel or stay away from toxic people because being around them feels unpleasant. When someone is experiencing tumultuous emotions and find it hard to calm and control themselves, it leads to displaying unpleasant behavior. Consciously changing that behavior needs to be learnt over time to better respond to erratic behavior. Regular occurrence of such behavior is definitely alarming, and people need to realize that this is something they need to work on.

Importance of Emotional Stability

Emotional stability has a direct connection with our relationships. To trust your loved one or your partner is of prime importance in a successful relationship. That trust factor can only come when the other counterpart is emotionally stable and does not react erratically. Conflicts occur in every relationship, but emotional stability is a factor that is crucial to solving those conflicts in the best of ways. Emotionally stable people can sort out matters by talking to each other and getting to the root cause of the issue through effective communication. Conversely, certain words can trigger conflict and make it spiral into something completely unneeded. So, here, emotional stability is of paramount importance.

When people are emotionally stable, they can progress together and make their relationship work out in the best way possible. Emotional stability brings that "feel good" factor into a relationship, making the relationship thrive.

A study conducted on this shows that emotional stability has a direct relationship to an individual's happiness. Happy people attract other happy people, eventually leading to successful relationships.

As happy people, we can have great relationships based on mutual trust and cooperation. No one likes being around toxic people. At the end of the day, we all want to lead peaceful and happy lives, which can only happen when we surround ourselves with happy people.

Toxic Traits

According to Mental Health America, 84% of women and 75% of men have reported having at least one toxic friend in their lives.

Being around toxic people is exhausting because it feels like they drain all of your energy. They subtly damage us, without us even realizing the effect that they are having on us.

To minimize the impact of toxic people, it is critical to understand what toxic traits are and how we can tell a toxic person apart from someone who's not.

Common Traits of Toxic People

Often, we can also be toxic, not realizing that the problem lies in us. So, that makes it all the more important to understand what toxic traits are.

Here are some of the traits of toxic people:

Manipulative Behavior

Toxic people can get what they want by making others believe what they say. They can convince others and use them according to their own wishes. They are able to do this by smartly twisting their words in a way that helps them get away with it without you ever realizing it. To do this, they often use emotional blackmail to get away with it.

Why Do They Do this?

Toxic people usually have ulterior motives behind what they are saying. Say, if a friend wants to hang out with you, they can just ask if you're free over the weekend. On the other hand, a toxic friend can tell you that if you don't meet them, they won't talk to you for the rest of the week. They can even bring emotions into the conversation, telling you to meet them if you love or care for them.

Negativity About Everything

Toxic people have the ability to find something negative in positive things as well. Their approach to life is very pessimistic, so they cannot see the bright side of things. This approach tends to drain others of their high spirits and could create doubt in their minds.

Judgmental Thinking

Toxic people are highly judgmental. They don't embrace things or people in their authentic selves unless they approve of it from their own lens. They see things in black and white and tend to criticize everything they disapprove of. Being around judgmental people is very uncomfortable because you just cannot be yourself around them. They always make you conscious of yourself.

Inability To Control Their Anger

Toxic people almost always seem to have very low control over their anger. Lashing out at others is something that toxic people often do. Being around toxic people makes you feel like you're walking on eggshells because you never know what might tick them off.

Self-Centered

Toxic people are mostly ones who only care for themselves. These people's lives revolve around themselves and do not show concern for anyone else around them. They use the *"I"* word because they care most about themselves. Considering the other person's point of view is not important to them at all.

Controlling Behavior

This is, in fact, the most dangerous trait of toxic people. They often want to control what the other person does. Being around such people can literally make one feel caged because they take your freedom from you and make you subject yourself to their will.

They Make Others Feel Bad About Themselves

This is a typical trait of a toxic person. They make others feel bad about themselves by passing unneeded comments about their clothing, body, height, or anything that makes the other feel bad. They often also tend to downplay others' achievements in life. This is again a thing that makes them feel 'superior' to the other person.

The "Fantastic" Mr. A

To have more clarity on this, I'll give the example of a troubled individual, Mr. A. He has been struggling with his personality problems for a long time. He has a repeated pattern of failing relationships in life due to that. Mr. A is an argumentative, closed-minded, narcissistic, and broken person. Over time, he has developed a very emotionally unstable personality. For him to interact with people without offending the other person in one way or another is nearly impossible, mainly due to his way of reacting.

Mr. A's wife left him due to the everyday quarrels over the minutest things. He was married to her for over ten years, but there was only a certain point where she could bear his continuous tantrums and lack of empathy. His wife was, in fact, a very reasonable person who tried to make their relationship work.

But sadly, Mr. A was extremely resistant to change, which was the root cause of his failing relationship. His children tend to avoid him because they think he is extremely unpleasant to be around. He continuously tries to boss them around by telling them what they should do. He tries to control his children's lives, but they do not appreciate that.

His coworkers do not enjoy his company since he gets into useless conversations that almost always lead to offending someone. His bosses have a hard time getting work done by him because he almost always questions everyone's way of doing things. Accepting someone else's point of view that is different from his own is something he really struggles with. The pinnacle of his anger is seen when he beats a man on the streets after getting into an argument with him, to the point that he has to be rushed to the hospital due to minor injuries. In short, it can be seen that Mr. A is an ideal example of a very toxic person. People do not like being around him due to the negativity he embodies, which is the root cause of his failing relationships in life.

If I ask you whether or not you would want to date Mr. A, we all know what the answer will be. No one likes to be around a person who can drain them of energy they have. Giving off a positive vibe is essential to attract others around you. Someone like Mr. A is disliked, mainly because of his personality and the lack of control over his emotions.

The Mr. A's in Our Lives

Many of us have come across people like Mr. A in life, who everyone wants to stay away from. When such people see that others repel them, they become even more adamant about staying the way they are, which again brings us back to the point I mentioned earlier: this is a vicious cycle. Toxic people fail to embrace change and get stuck in that cycle. Coming out of this becomes something that is near impossible for them to do. No one likes to date people who are unpleasant. When people date, they do so to get the companionship they desire. However, when you date a toxic person, they also rob you of your confidence by continuously complaining about something or the other or finding faults in your being, which is exactly what Mr. A did.

The conversation is always about them and never about you, which can be very frustrating at most times.

Love and being loved are beautiful feelings. Toxic people take all the good out of love through repeated and unnecessary actions. They make love feel complicated when it really isn't.

One of my favorite quotes about love is this one:

"Love is always patient and kind. It is never jealous. Love is never boastful or conceited. It is never rude or selfish. It does not take offense and is not resentful. Love takes no pleasure in other people's sins, but delights in the truth. It is always ready to excuse, to trust, to hope, and to endure whatever comes."

— 1 Corinthians 13:4-7.

Toxic people don't let love remain remotely close to this. Instead, they tarnish the essence of love with the toxicity that they embody.

Becoming Better than Mr. A

To have meaningful relationships is life's essence, which is why I am writing this book. I want this book to guide all who want to have healthy relationships in life. Also, this book can help all those with toxic tendencies overcome them and become better versions of themselves, which is key to healthy relationships.

With a little bit of work on ourselves, we can understand our emotions in a much better way and understand the commitment to change that is needed for us to let go of the negativity that resides within us.

My main motivation for writing this book is to help all those struggling with learning about their mistakes. We all are human, and we all make mistakes. What is important is that we embrace those and be open to letting go of what makes us undesirable to others.

Human beings tend to fall prey to toxic characteristics. However, we can drive the change within, take baby steps toward becoming better versions of ourselves, and water our relationships for them to bloom.

CHAPTER.2

Moving Beyond Toxicity

Self-awareness leads to the road to self-discovery. We've talked about what toxic traits are and the detrimental effects these can have on our lives. We all have our flaws, but what is most important is that we work on them.

It is nearly impossible for someone to change their entire personality, it can evolve and get more refined, but the basic traits of your personality do not change. Sure, aspects of one's personality can be changed over time, with diligent efforts and consistency, but the overall change is limited.

However, some traits in humans are habitual, such as helping others out of kindness or being toxic just because you have a habit of getting other people's attention that way. Needless to say, most of these are habitual responses that can be changed over time. It is imperative that we change our toxic habits because it's inevitable for us not to affect our surroundings and the loved ones around us with those toxic habits or traits. Just like how Mr. A's attitude was undesirable and disrespectful to the people around him, your toxic traits would also have the same effect. These traits make us socially undesirable and unpleasant. If you think you have any toxic traits, then you first have to identify them and, after that, have to work on them.

Not working on your toxic can sabotage your happiness and relationships and negatively affect your health.

In society, playing the blame game is very easy; it's not uncommon for us to blame society, our friends, our partner, or other personal conditions for all the bad things happening to us. It is only out of habit that we blame external factors. It comes as part of our natural instincts to look on the outside for the problems.

All these may contribute to our lackluster moments, but once we realize that the problem resides within, we need to solve it ourselves. For if we ourselves do not highlight our problems, there cannot be any change.

Working on Toxic Traits

We have discussed how important it is to work on your toxic traits and what might happen if you fail to work on them. What we haven't talked about is how to work on your toxic traits. It might not be as simple as its sounds, but one step at a time is key.

Identify Your Toxic Traits

Identifying what toxic traits you have is the first step to being able to work on them. You cannot work on your problems if you do not know what the problem is. Therefore, it is important that you reflect on your daily routine and identify any toxic traits that we discussed in the last chapter. Start by making a list of all the toxic traits that you have.

You might have noticed these in yourself, or your significant other or other people around you might have put these forward. It is never easy to find flaws in oneself, but if you have a drive for change, then nothing is impossible. The important thing here is that we must be able to change.

For example, you might feel you're too self-centered, controlling, or even manipulative. First, find out what these traits are and then;

Take Accountability

This is of the utmost importance when it comes to our journey of growth. It is only when we take full ownership of our toxic traits that we are able to better understand ourselves and acknowledge what is going wrong compared to when we actively choose to ignore a negative trait that can be very toxic and damaging in the long run.

For example, if you think you are very controlling and make your partner uncomfortable, acknowledge and accept it first. If you do not do that, you might take steps that could break the relationship or harm your partner. More often than not, we find it hard to be in a place where we can accept our flaws. That is because we are in denial, thinking we could never exhibit these behaviors. Unfortunately, this harms us and our many relationships in life. Remember, toxic traits are mostly habits we develop in response to a certain situation. For instance, you might feel that you have a certain toxic trait because of your circumstances, like being brought up in an abusive household or being hurt in a past relationship. What matters the most is acknowledging the toxic traits, owning up to them, and finding ways to get past them healthily. Realizing things can take time, and that is natural. But once you do, you can begin your journey of self-improvement by;

Changing Your Ways

Once you know your toxic traits and accept them, start working on them one at a time. For example, if you have identified your controlling nature, the next time you find yourself in a situation where the controlling part of your personality is taking over, you can,

- Make deliberate efforts to push it down

- Try to remain quite

- End the argument or excuse yourself,

- Try listening to what the other person has to say and;

- Do the opposite of what you would naturally do.

That really helps in terms of helping you see the other side of the story and gives you other ways of dealing with this.

Toxic habits have their ways of pulling you back. You need to make sure that doesn't happen by making conscious efforts in that direction. Even if you encounter mental resistance, push through because only you can bring about the change you wish to see in yourself.

Get Impartial Opinion

Ask for help from others around you. Go to people who know you well as your partner, and ask them to highlight your toxic traits. Sit with them and ask them to stop you if you show any toxic behavior.

Another thing that you can do is to seek professional health. Asking a therapist can also be a great idea. Ask them how you can improve, and you can get useful tips from there too. Then, taking their advice, you can adapt and change. In fact, I would say that it would be better that you go to a professional for help as they know what they are dealing with and would have dealt with similar cases before.

Be Consistent

As I mentioned earlier, change does not come easy. It takes a lot of time and, most importantly, consistency. You cannot expect yourself to just wake up one day as a completely different and changed individual. To be the best version of yourself, you need to change your ways of dealing with things. A quick guide includes:

- Starting somewhere

- Identifying what you need to change

- Working on a solution or a program

- Continuing with the program

The important thing in all this is that you keep following the program. Even if it seems hard, keep going, and I assure you, you will eventually get there. As human beings, we are often bogged down when the result of the change is invisible.

As creatures of habit, we want things to be done sequentially and quickly. Unfortunately, things don't work like that in the real world. The results of change are only seen very slowly, over time, as we continue to progress. Whatever goals you set for yourself, do so with the intention of sticking to them for a long period of time.

As social creatures, we are naturally conditioned to develop relationships. We long for connection, but our toxic traits can come in the way of that, eventually ruining our happiness and lives. Toxic relationships can be deadly. In fact, they do more harm than we can ever imagine. The scars of toxic relationships stay with people for a long time. So when a toxic trait starts to harm your relationship, you might become a burden on your partner.

Am I a Burden on My Partner?

I have noticed so many failing relationships around me, resulting from one person becoming codependent and ultimately becoming a burden on the other. This is detrimental to not only your relationship's health but also your health. Extreme dependency on your partner can make them feel caged, and the relationship becomes more like a burden.

Being a burden to your partner is, in fact, one of the most unappealing things to the other person because they may start feeling like you have become an added liability to them. Having your own interests, feelings, and opinions is very important for them to view you as an independent and strong-headed individual. Most people enter into relationships often expecting their partners to meet all of their needs, be it social connection, support, or sexual desires. Some even expect their partners to understand their needs and then fulfill them. This is something that is very emotionally immature and irresponsible. Your partner is not liable for taking responsibility for your needs. You have to know,

- Your needs

- What it is you expect from the relationship

- Understanding your partner's limitations

- Making sure that you pull your own weight

- Helping your partner when they are in a pinch

Basically, you have to understand that your partner is different from you and wouldn't necessarily like the same things you do. For example,

If you like going to concerts, your partner might not.

You might love partying out at night; your partner might not.

You might love cooking; your partner might not.

And you know what? It's perfectly okay.

That doesn't mean that you have to stop doing those things, or your partner must make a sacrifice. Start doing what YOU like to do, and don't expect your partner to be with you through all of it.

You are separate individuals with distinct likes and dislikes. Embrace all of that, and do what makes you happy. Loving your partner doesn't mean that you only accept what you like about them. They are their own individuals, and you have to accept both their good and poor qualities. You cannot expect someone else to be responsible for your happiness. It can be a real turn-off for the other person if they are always conscious of their actions when they are around you.

When in a happy relationship, most people usually feel free as they feel that their partners wouldn't judge them. Your feelings are valid, and your choices are yours. Own up to them, and work for them with your own hands. If you make others work for you, you WILL become a burden.

You need to realize that apart from having a life together, you both have your own lives and must also live that separately from each other. It is fine to desire someone who shares the same ideas as you, but at the same time, there is not a single person on this planet who would share all your qualities.

Sure, they might be similar, but they will never be the same as your personality, and your qualities are what make you, you. Forcing your ideas on your partner or expecting them to share your problems is, in all honesty, unfair to them. In the beginning, they might put up with you and support you in your hardships, as they should.

But after a point, if you do nothing or do not try your best to get out of the predicament that you find yourself in, then your partner will abandon you, and it would not have been their fault. To be independent is synonymous with being attractive and emotionally and mentally healthy.

Your partner will like you more when he or she sees how opinionated you are and how you have your likes and dislikes that you like to take care of yourself. Problems are around all of us, and everyone faces difficulties, but this doesn't mean that anyone else has to solve them for you.

Sure, they can and should help, but expecting them to solve the problem for you is where the trouble begins. If you think you or your partner is putting all their load on you, change your ways and be forward about it.

Another extremely important thing is to hold your feelings in high regard, understand their importance, and make your partner know that you value your emotions. Emotional independence is important for a healthy relationship.

Don't carry your wounds with you, but know that if you feel a certain way, you need to acknowledge it and then do something about it to move on from there. Only when you value your feelings yourself will your partner too. So respect yourself, and a healthy relationship will just follow.

So, in short;

- Do not burden your partner with problems

- Do not try to force your ideas on them (sharing is not forcing)

- Let them live life the way they want

- Share your problems with them but do not expect them to solve your problems for you

The Importance of Being Driven

An internal drive and the desire to achieve in life make a person stand out from the rest. When you are internally driven and have specifically laid out goals ahead of yourself, your chances of success in life naturally become much higher, and others around you also begin to view you positively.

Most people say, *"Follow your dreams,"* but not everyone does. Dreams make life worth living in the sense that they give you purpose.

A quote from Oscar Wilde that I absolutely love is: *"'To live' is the rarest thing in the world. Most people just exist."*

When you have goals ahead of yourself, you become someone who has something to look forward to in life that you are working for. You have something to which you have directed your energies. Not only is this an extremely positive trait for yourself as a person, but it also has a trickle-down effect on your relationships. When you have an achievement-oriented and driven partner, you naturally tend to look up to them and value them for the goals they have set for themselves in life. You view them positively because you can see that they have a purpose to live, and their life has plans. I personally feel that amongst all other traits that make a person seem desirable, are,

- Self-dependency

- Achievement orientation

- Being internally driven

When others value you for you, they look up to you and place you in high regard. Even for a successful relationship, it is important that your partner values you and looks at you as someone who knows where they are headed in life.

I remember I once had a friend who was one of the very few people in my life I saw as a real example of being in a successful relationship. She was one of the most driven people in life. She owned a hair salon and was ambitious about going places with it. She set targets for her salon and set out to achieve those. Her partner valued her for her and knew that he wasn't the only thing she had in life to look forward to.

Just that feeling of being with someone so achievement-oriented made her partner value her, which led to them having a very successful relationship.

By being driven, I don't necessarily mean to imply having a well-planned career or a lot of wealth, per se.

What I mean is that a person should have goals in life. They should have something that they look forward to and something that they aspire to be. Others look up to these characteristics in a person.

Your dream can be as simple as helping those in need or maybe owning a small home-run bakery. It can be anything that you aspire to do and love to do. As long as you have a road to follow, others will look to you with admiration and inspiration.

Developing an Attractive Persona

An attractive persona automatically makes a person successful in their relationships. Everyone wants to be liked, but most people don't understand that this comes from you watering your own personality.

An attractive persona comes from developing a character that others love. This is why some people can make a lasting impression while others do not.

What makes a person stand out?

a)   Being self-sufficient

b)   Having clear career goals

c)   Hobbies

d)   Great lifestyle choices

e)   Having a positive attitude in life

These things are what make one appear attractive to the other person. Often, people try to copy others or become someone they're not. While they might think that others won't notice, this is easily detectable by those close to them who know their habits. People who keep forging certain new characteristics almost every other day or week start seeming very fake. Anyone can tell that this is not their real selves but a version they are trying to put forth to the rest.

To develop an attractive persona, you need to work on yourself and have a positive outlook on life. For that, you need to have dreams, and then you need to work hard to chase those dreams to get where you want in life. When your partner sees how strong-willed and motivated you are, they will automatically love you more because of the person they see growing and maturing. Likewise, when you water your personality, you grow to become someone that others love. So successful relationships come more from personal growth than anything else.

Attractive Personality Traits

Here are some personality traits that can help you blossom into a very appealing person, which eventually also affects your relationships in life:

Confidence

When you're confident in your skin, you radiate positivity and make the other person feel good. So people like to affiliate themselves with confident people because it also makes them feel great about themselves. Joseph Burgo, a psychotherapist, said, *"High self-esteem is sexy, provided it doesn't veer into narcissistic self-absorption."*

Interest

To have particular interests is something that can tell others that you have a very strong personality. People like to be with others who have interests in things. They make others curious to know more about them. You shouldn't have to sell yourself to others. They should understand that you have very particular interests and they should themselves ask you about them.

Optimism

To have a positive outlook in life is also something important. Negativity breeds negativity, so always look for the happy things in life and focus on the good in most situations.

Friendliness

You should always appear friendly to the other person. People should want to come to you and talk to you because you give them that vibe. Cultivating these traits over time should not be very hard. Slowly but surely, you will get there.

Healing From Past Traumas

Trauma is a psychological and physiological response to distressing or disturbing events in one's life. These responses can manifest physically, emotionally, and psychologically, leading to a decreased quality of life. Additionally, it also causes a person to develop unhealthy coping mechanisms.

These can lead to further problems such as self-loathing, creating a vicious cycle where they keep drowning in sorrow and negative feelings while indulging in unhealthy coping mechanisms to overcome them. This becomes very problematic.

How one deals with trauma differs greatly from person to person. People who cannot deal with traumas tend to suffer from them and seem unable to overcome them. No matter how hard they push, the trauma is embedded in their lives. They lose any sense of security as well. Just like how coping mechanisms differ greatly, recovery from trauma is also difficult and different for everyone. Some do, and some don't. The National Council has estimated that around 70% of American adults have experienced at least one traumatic event. To truly overcome trauma, we must understand how it affects our lives. This is why we must consciously try to understand and overcome trauma, no matter how challenging it seems.

Effect of Trauma on Our Lives and Relationships Traumatized people aren't their usual selves. They usually feel down, are hypervigilant or depressed, and have a negative outlook on life. While traumatized people need support from others the most, their depression and negative viewpoints tend to make them less likely to receive that support from their friends and family. The trickle-down effect on the other person tends to repel others.

Coping with trauma healthily is necessary because it can compromise our relationships. Trauma impairs our ability to function properly, which can affect our bonds. Close friends and partners are the most immediate people affected by the side effects one experiences.

Certain traumatic experiences can affect a person's relationships. Examples include the death of a loved one, childhood abuse, emotional abuse, neglect, and more. Since the perpetrators of that traumatic event can be people close to them, it leads to a person having trust issues, feeling betrayed in a relationship, making the other person very uncomfortable, and more.

Survivors often feel vulnerable and exposed. A traumatized person tends to feel shame, guilt, or even anger, which reflects in the relationship.

Dealing with Trauma

Something commonly seen is that many people tend to suppress past traumas to move on. I cannot stress enough how unhealthy this is. Suppressing trauma isn't the solution because you are not acknowledging that it was there at all. This can, in fact, lead to trauma snowballing.

When people suppress trauma, the bottled feelings do not go away. Instead, they fester and find new outlets. It can also lead to developing unhealthy coping mechanisms such as alcohol addiction, drug abuse, and more. Therefore, it is necessary to deal with the trauma in a healthy manner.

So, if you're considering dealing with the trauma, here are a few healthy ways that you can do just that.

Acknowledge and Recognize the Trauma

The first step is to acknowledge the trauma. Unfortunately, victims of childhood abuse often dismiss their trauma by pretending it never happened at all. Sometimes, they even succumb to feelings of guilt, which can be very unhealthy.

Trauma does not follow any hierarchy, so comparisons only make it worse. Accepting the trauma for what it was is how we get over it.

So accept your trauma, and understand what it was. Only then can healing begin.

Reclaim Control

What happened in your life does not define you, nor does it play a part in shaping your future. Acting as a perpetual victim leads you to make the wrong choices, which negatively affects your life.

You are in the driving seat of your life and in full control of what happens. So take control, and steer yourself in the direction you wish to. Don't make yourself a subject of circumstance because you aren't.

For example, if your ex-lover left you, don't lose yourself to that. It may be tough, but you must remember that letting that event control you will also dictate your future relationships. A thing of the past is something gone. Do not let that affect what is yet to come.

I cannot stress enough that all of this completely depends on one's mental health. You are the only one who can convince yourself to look on the brighter side of things. Know that these feelings of helplessness will only make you feel worse.

So you need to make a conscious effort in that direction.

Seek Support

If you have to, seek professional help. Sometimes, the stress that comes from trauma can be crippling.

Grief and depression can entirely take over. If that is interfering with daily affairs, then it is not normal.

You need to seek help from an expert who can guide you in this situation. Unfortunately, people tend to shy away from getting professional help.

This is mainly because of the stigma that is attached to it.

Make yourself a priority. If you feel like seeking help can be better for you, don't second guess it. Call a professional. You can also join certain support groups. Hearing about other people's trauma can help you understand that you are not alone and life does get better.

Do Not Isolate

Many times, trauma survivors tend to isolate themselves from others. This is something that comes instinctively. However, isolation only worsens things. It puts you in a headspace where it is only you and your feelings, which can make you feel like you're drowning.

That can be very draining. However, this doesn't mean that you should be surrounding yourself with people needlessly. It just implies that the comfort you get from feeling engaged with others can help you cope much better.

The True Meaning of Acceptance and Letting Go

Accepting your trauma means coming to terms with the fact that something bad happened. Now that it is over, you need to let it go.

For example, if you've had a heartbreak, then accepting it means telling yourself that it didn't work out because the two of you were incompatible and the other person did not feel like they connected with you well.

Does that hurt?

Of course, it does.

But understanding the situation and making a conscious effort to let go of it is healthy. It gives you back power. Acceptance means that you have decided you are going to let it go.

Of course, this doesn't happen overnight. It takes many steps that will pave your way to the top. But let me assure you that you will surely make it with consistent efforts.

The Dynamics of Modern Relationships

The technological age has made relationships rather straightforward and simple. Ghosting is very common. No one has to give explanations. People can disappear whenever they want to. But for people who take these things to heart, it can be very hurtful and result in emotional trauma. Unfortunately, in the world that we live in today, we see so many people stricken by grief when a relationship doesn't work out well.

Heartbreaks can be traumatizing, but we must realize that it is extremely unhealthy to take things personally. When someone ghosts you, the problem doesn't lie with you; it could be with them.

When you're ghosted, just understand that this was the easiest way out of the situation for the other person.

No explanations.

No worries.

They just leave.

Taking this personally can be detrimental to your mental health. There are numerous reasons why this might have happened.

They could just not be serious about the relationship or not want a commitment this early. On the other hand, they might have been cheating on someone or dealing with their over-abandonment issues that subsequently affect your relationship. Whatever the reason, the universe always aligns what's best for you, which are often blessings in disguise. Know that there can be numerous reasons for their behavior, and you taking it personally will only affect you and exhaust you emotionally.

Don't give others that control over you because it is not healthy. Instead, learn to let go, move on, and take things a little lighter. You owe that to yourself.

Remember, we are all going through something. So don't be too hard on others, either. Don't hold grudges against people, and let others be.

If something bad happened to you because of another person, forgive them. Just know that they made a decision owing to their own circumstances, and they stuck by it. So don't ruin your life because of it. Let it go as a decision they made for themselves. You cannot let yourself be a subject of their decision because one thing to remember is that it is not personal.

Acknowledgment and Acceptance are Key

For survivors of self-trauma, even simple moments of self-kindness can be quite challenging. However, when people tread the road to self-healing and cautiously start to become a little more hopeful about returning to some semblance of interaction with others, they are mostly concerned about divulging.

On the path to healing, we must understand how the process can be slow and steady, but surely, we can get there. The key is acceptance; acknowledging that something has happened to us and making conscious efforts to heal is important here.

You need to tell yourself that what happened to you was not your fault. You were never responsible for it, so you must stop holding yourself accountable for it too.

Yes, it happened.

Yes, it hurt you.

Yes, it still does affect you.

But it cannot dictate your life further and shape your future relationships. YOU are important. When you value yourself, you are learning to let go of things. Know that you can and you will.

With a little self-determination and control, you can conquer and heal!

CHAPTER.4

Hope

During hardships, it is difficult to believe there will be any semblance of normalcy in our lives again. As a result, we tend to lose hope, further pulling us down the abyss we are facing.

Whether it be the loss of a loved one, a failed relationship, or being unable to achieve our goals, it can be pretty disheartening. Circumstances like these tend to weigh us down and make us feel despair and lose hope.

Hope can be found in an external source, but the strongest hope is the one that comes from within. It comes from the gut, the drive that motivates us to take action. Yet relying on external sources is not the way to go about it because that means that your hope is finite. Instead, we need to look for it within. It fuels and energizes us to keep moving ahead in life. Refocusing on one's dream might not always be easy, but holding on to hope is imperative to ensure it happens.

A famous saying from Eleanor Roosevelt that I hold close to my heart is,

"When you think you're at the end of your rope, tie a knot and hang on."

I love how this quote shows us the importance of looking for hope even when there is no way forward.

Why is Hope Important?

In our lives, hope gives us a sense of purpose. It allows us to keep moving despite all odds. It helps us cope with the atrocities of life. It motivates us to look above and beyond what's gone wrong and reinforces the belief that life will change. Hope allows us to;

Stay Motivated

Just the idea that better times are yet to come or are just around the corner would give us the motivation to move forward. This willingness can help us drive against the strong currents and remain steadfast in what we do.

Look To the Future

Hope helps us understand that the grass is not always greener on the other side. It makes us believe that everything will turn out for the best if we just hold on. It helps one visualize a better future to keep going and looking for better things to come. We succeed only if we view things from a fresh perspective.

Keeps Us Going

The possibility of a better future can give us the drive we need to keep going, despite major curveballs. Hope allows you to stop having a passive approach to life and move toward an active one. We need to have hope to know that we will rise, despite all the odds. When a relationship fails, we tend to lose hope. We drown in sorrow and cannot entirely comprehend why it failed. In most situations, we may blame ourselves and develop a gloomy outlook for the future.

Hanging on to hope in such a situation would mean telling ourselves that maybe life has something better in store for us.

The concept of hope often intermingles with other ideas, which does not help us understand it well. For example, people often think that hope and optimism are synonymous, but are they the same thing?

Is Hope the Same as Optimism?

No. Hope and optimism are two different emotions that overlap but are distinct and different.

Optimism is broader and focuses on positive future outcomes as a whole. So optimism is more like an approach to life that everyone should have to have a positive outlook.

Hope, on the other hand, comes from within and is mostly related to personal matters. It directly relates to a person's experiences in life. Additionally, it mainly involves beliefs that people have about themselves. It is the inner strength that they look for when things get tough.

While hope and optimism relate to positive states of mind, they are different regarding mental well-being.

Having a Positive Outlook on Life

To cope with life's difficulties, we must have a positive outlook. We must understand that life is not easy for most people. A lot of people have to struggle to get what they want. However, the will to move forward, even when faced with setbacks, resides within us.

Whenever we encounter a challenging life situation, we tend to think we are doomed. This approach is very unhealthy.

When people believe in such things, it sabotages their effort, subconsciously making them more likely to stay stuck in a horrible situation. So, if life is getting difficult or if something is bothering you, try the following:

- Do not let it weigh you down.

- Do not tell yourself that you are doomed.

- Think of the different ways you can get out of the current situation.

- Always look to the people less fortunate than you for perspective, rather than those who are luckier and more successful.

Just like happy moments, we have sad or challenging circumstances in life. All that is required of us in such situations is to find the courage and willpower to move on, despite all odds.

In tough times, we need to find the strength to keep pushing. We need to realize our true potential. Of course, that isn't easy, but the whole point is to keep progressing.

You must have come across the famous saying, *"Where there is a will, there's a way."*

It essentially means that when people are determined to do something, they find the means to do it, one way or the other. They overcome the obstacles that come their way. If you fail an exam but are determined to pass the next one, no one can stop you from achieving that.

Constantly remind yourself that you are in the driving seat.

You can change the direction of your life any time you want to.

A very dear friend of mine lost the love of her life to cancer. I could see how broken she was. She didn't talk to anyone and shut herself off from the world. I could see that she had lost the will to live.

Unfortunately, the loss she experienced wasn't allowing her to look beyond it. It took her a good three months to fully accept what had happened. But I applaud her willingness to move on. She picked herself up and opened up her own bakery. She put her art to good use and became a pastry chef. She indulged in activities that made her happy. She looked past her sorrows, and I could see her blossoming into someone great who found her strength in herself.

Today, I see her as someone very successful. She is one of the strongest women I know. She is also a motivational speaker and gives speeches on how our strength always resides within. It is up to us to find it in different ways and at times.

Hope and the Possibility of Something Better

Always remember that there is a better tomorrow. We need to understand that the best is yet to come. With that thought in mind, we can channel our energy in the right way. We need to think of our future with positivity.

Different challenges will come our way because life is neither a bed of roses nor an open road. Life is more like being stuck in traffic where the road ahead is blocked, and you have to crawl forward. Of course, this won't always be easy amidst all the chaos. But that's the real challenge. Look past the bad days and keep going, no matter what.

With hope also comes persistence.

When we don't give up hope, it transforms into persistence – the force that pushes us to do our best and move ahead. Of course, the possibility of things not always turning out the way we want is always there.

But you have to understand that we need to keep moving. There will always be difficulties, but the hope of a better future will always keep you going. Only when we live in the present and think of the future can we live a fulfilling life!

Hope helps us become better people because it helps us channel the negativity within us by making us look at the brighter side.

Hope and Toxic Traits

We have already discussed toxic traits and how they affect our lives. Hope has a direct connection to us dealing with our toxic traits. For example, if someone is manipulative, hope can help them change the situation. If someone abuses their power, then hope can help them understand how they don't have to suffer to get what is theirs; it will automatically come to them. Hope can instill positivity if they have a negative approach to life. They just need to channel their energy in the right direction.

So, on the whole, hope drives us to live positively. It empowers us by helping us look at things from a positive perspective, which is necessary to overcome our sorrowful times.

Do you know anyone who hasn't gone through tough times in their life?

No, right!

Everyone faces challenges, and these help us grow in different ways. We can look at the brighter side of things and understand that a better future is yet to come. We just need to find the courage to move past these difficulties. Therefore, it is important to be hopeful to reach your goals in life.

Michelle Obama once said,

"You may not always have a comfortable life, and you will not always be able to solve all of the world's problems at once but don't ever underestimate the importance you can have because history has shown us that courage can be contagious and hope can take on a life of its own."

I love the power of this saying in terms of how it describes courage. We all need to have hope and, at the same time, try to have a positive outlook.

CHAPTER.5

The Growth Process in Overcoming Toxicity and its Outcome

Toxicity takes a significant toll on one's mental health. It is imperative that we focus on growth and self-improvement. However, that is easier said than done; the process is long and challenging. Healing takes time and a lot of consistent effort. Working on personal growth is also very subjective. There isn't a specific formula to help you become a better version of yourself. However, there are some things you can try that can help increase your chances of succeeding.

Stages of Self-Improvement and Growth

The stages of self-growth can be seen as a six-step journey that increases the chances of success. Following these steps can make the growth process simpler and more straightforward.

Step 1: Unknowing

This is the stage where we are still unaware of where and what we lack. In some cases, this stage is also characterized by denial or a lack of acceptance. We follow the path of willful ignorance, which further adds to our mounting problems. Ignorance is, in fact, not 'bliss,' as ignoring your problems only results in further complications. To avoid that, we go to the second stage.

Step 2: Awareness

This is the stage where personal growth begins. We awaken to reality and understand the facts, realizing where everything went wrong. Therefore, gaining a deeper understanding of ourselves is integral to growth. Knowing one's self allows us to plan for the future and set boundaries as we become aware of our limits. After learning more about yourself, you can move to the next step of acceptance.

Step 3: Acceptance

This is a stage characterized by a healthy sense of self-love. Once we are aware of ourselves, we finally realize and understand the toxic traits we need to work on. For most, this can be scary and uncomfortable, but to change, we first need to accept our faults. We are all humans and make mistakes, so it is nothing wrong if you are in the wrong. However, once we realize something wrong with us, it becomes our responsibility to amend our ways.

Step 4: Responsibility

At this stage, we take matters into our own hands and decide to move toward positive change that is imperative to healthy growth. We realize that our actions affect others around us, which isn't acceptable. Accepting your flaws or mistakes isn't the only way; you must work toward fixing all your problems. By being responsible for our actions, we learn to live proactively and make decisions for the best. We feel empowered at this stage and understand how we can change for the better.

Step 5: Application

Once we have taken full responsibility, it becomes much easier to apply that. We need self-discipline, motivation, and focus on applying this to our lives. Behind our aim, there need to be solid and well-aligned goals. We need to work toward where we want to see ourselves, ideally as people who can work in the best of ways toward goal attainment.

Step 6: Purpose

At this stage, we learn how to keep going strong and achieve our goals. A strong mindset and deeply cultivated habits can help us develop into the mirror image of what we visualize for ourselves. Finally, we get a purpose and direction that we can follow. Thus, striving to do our best can help us achieve what we want.

To become better individuals, we must ensure that we have fulfilling relationships in life. The road to self-improvement can help prepare us for the dating world, transforming us into someone who exudes positive energy and growth. Remember, a healthy individual fuels a sparking relationship.

With self-awareness and emotional intelligence, we not only understand how to channel our own emotions, but at the same time, we also understand how to handle people better and more comfortably. Putting ourselves in the shoes of others becomes easier when we are empathetic toward others.

You have probably heard the phrase,

"You are what you attract."

This stresses the importance of healing from toxicity. It means that when people are negative in one way or the other, they attract negativity, which again puts them in a vicious cycle. This makes it very hard to focus on the good in life. So, overcoming toxicity is crucial to mental well-being and healthy relationships.

If we are manipulative, we tend to give off that vibe, further attracting negative energy. So watering our healthy traits and teaching habits that are good for our mental well-being can help us tread the road to healthier relationships.

Importance of Personal Growth

Our transformational journey is very personal to our different selves. We understand ourselves best and are aware of how we can change for the better. To blossom into a better person is a predicament that appears extremely daunting to most, but when you see what you want in life, the road that leads to that becomes much clearer. Personal growth can help us become better versions of ourselves, attract positive energy and, in turn, affect our quality of life.

A healthy relationship is a union of two happy souls. But for that to happen, we first need to grow as individuals and become better versions of ourselves. Successful relationships reflect the true persona of an individual. Only after a person has healed on the inside can they have positive relationships, fuel positive energy, and live a healthy life. Remember, the only thing that is constant in life is change. Therefore, we need to understand the importance of evolving as people and blossoming into better individuals. With personal growth as our primary focus, we can understand how important it is to change ourselves for the better.

Brooks Atkinson, a prize-winning journalist, pointed out what stagnation is in his eyes,

"The most fatal illusion is the settled point of view. Since life is growth and motion, a fixed point of view kills anybody who has one...."

I love how Atkinson focuses on the dire need to change and evolve. Anyone who has a fixed point of view becomes stagnant in life. If you made a mistake in a relationship in the past due to your toxic traits, you need to work on that and become better so that it doesn't affect future relationships. While lifelong learning and personal growth are mantras for many today, they rarely ever translate into actions, leading to all the problems.

Personal Growth and Relationships

Understanding and catering to our needs can make us better versions of ourselves. A successful relationship does not involve two people relying on each other to fulfill their needs. But in fact, it involves people healing from their toxic traits and then creating a fulfilling union for both of them. If you have specific needs, you must work toward ensuring those are fulfilled. It is extremely wrong to expect them to fulfill those for you. Expecting from your significant other can be a real turn-off for them and might deter the relationship's success as well. To live a fulfilled life, we must understand ourselves first fully. Only when we do that can we know its importance for a healthy life.

We, as human beings, are subjects of emotion. But do we know how to handle our emotions well?

Well, not most people.

Dealing with the Emotional Self

Ever been in a position where the storm of depression is taking you over?

Or when you're so angry that you can't function?

Or when you just go numb?

All of us experience these emotions, but it is more important to understand how we can channel them in the best ways and understand their importance. As human beings, we can sometimes fall prey to our emotions. But understanding them, directing our energies to overcome them, and channeling them into something else is what matters.

So then, what's the best way of dealing with our emotions?

The first and most important thing here is understanding the numbing behaviors. We must understand what exactly leads us to become different versions of ourselves. Even if we think our feelings can be irrational at times, we need to acknowledge and understand them first to deal with them. Sometimes, we can be too hard on ourselves. We judge ourselves for our feelings and sometimes even compare them to others. This is not healthy at all.

When you feel angry, don't feel bad about it. Instead, try to understand what is making you feel that way. Don't feel guilty, but understand how you can work toward solutions in the best possible way and channel your anger correctly. What may work for one person might not work for you, and vice versa. Maybe you could isolate yourself? Or do something that you like? Perhaps you could consciously shut your mind off and sleep for a while?

Remember, you know yourself best. Understand your emotions, acknowledge them, and then manage them. Know that expressing your feelings to a limited extent is not unhealthy. In fact, it is something that is much needed. Emotional growth can affect your personality and make you grow into someone very likable.

Emotional Growth and its Effect on Personality

Emotional evolution can make you more desirable to those around you. When you experience dynamic growth, you take responsibility for your emotions.

This means that you don't blame others for something that happens to you or when you feel a certain way. You blame yourself for what happens in light of the spirit of humility.

As a result, you become more action-oriented and start working out ways to improve the situation. Your approach to life becomes much more careful, and you understand how showing empathy and owning up to your mistakes is integral to success in life. You know that there can be situations in life that can make you highly vulnerable. You learn to understand how to work your way through them and not try to be 'perfect' at most times. You also tend to set healthy boundaries and realize how that can work in your best interest. When you grow this way emotionally, you become someone who gives off positive energy, thus becoming highly likable to people around you. People see you as mature and someone who understands how to channel their emotions.

Objectives of Personal Growth

Here are a few objectives of personal growth that can help you.

A clear sense of direction

Know what you want in life, your end goal, and why you want to reach it.

Improved work ethic

Instead of slacking off, try to work toward your set goal.

Better relationships

This doesn't only include your partner but also includes family and friends.

Increased productivity

Try working hard and as much as you can. Do not put things off until tomorrow; if you can do them tomorrow, you can do them today. Keeping these objectives in mind can help you set a clear path. They can help you better comprehend yourself and understand how the road to self-discovery and growth is not as challenging as it seems. It's one step at a time, and you will surely get there.

First, make your choices in life, and then own up to them. Like I said, you are in the driving seat of your life. Make all your efforts go in the right direction and evolve for the better. You will see how an objective-based approach will help you get where you want to be.

I mentioned earlier how hope is something that you need to look for internally. It comes from the internal motivation that you have. So look for that hope within yourself and tell yourself that life has much more for you in store than you thought.

Latch on to that, and success will be yours. You will be amazed to see how much positive energy you attract when you become a better version of yourself.

PART II
2nd Dimension: Mental Stability – As Thou Thinketh

Figuring Out the Signs

"There is a crack in everything, that's how the light gets in."

-Leonard Cohen

Everything is flawed, full of cracks. Yet those flaws and cracks make way for light and hope to come in. Similarly, no problem exists that doesn't have a solution. So even if the cracks are within you, they can be mended and pave the way for your growth.

Mental Stability

Mental stability isn't easily attainable; only a few can achieve it. Even those who appear stable on the outside can still suffer from turmoil within. Mental stability or mental health is a key component of a person's mind and constitutes how they behave with others around them.

Mental health is the absence of mental disorders or disabilities, but it has many more components that lead to a stable and sound mind. It includes our psychological, social, and emotional well-being. It affects how we think, go through our daily lives, interact with others, and handle the stresses that life throws at us. A mentally stable person would be able to;

1. Cope with the daily stress

2. Handle most of the difficulties of life

3. Understand their limits

4. Manage the crazy amount of load and stress

5. Know how to handle themselves

6. Work better and more efficiently

People know their limits and capabilities when they learn how to take on stress. They know how to work more productively and efficiently. As their work ethics improve, their work no longer takes a toll on them, burdening them with further stress.

When someone is not being burdened by their work and internal battles, they can better think of the people close to them. They expand their reach and look at the world with new eyes. As they view things from a new perspective, they get the urge to change them for the better, share their happiness with others, and contribute more to society.

Similarly, if a person doesn't know their limits or capabilities, they would keep crossing their boundaries and limits, further adding to their stress. A mentally stable person is like a star shining brightly in the night sky. They twinkle and guide others toward the light

Mental Instability

Mental instability is something that most people today suffer from. It is something that almost everybody has experienced at some point in their life, albeit with varying intensity.

There are some signs to look for in a person suffering from unstable mental health—namely, becoming socially awkward, constantly fighting with loved ones, doing drugs, body aches and pains, hearing voices, and feeling of helplessness. Suicidal thoughts or harming yourself, sleep issues, feeling lethargic, and being unable to perform daily tasks are also side effects of having mental problems.

Social Awkwardness

One sign of deteriorating mental health is a person pulling away from their usual activities by becoming socially awkward and distancing themselves from everyone. This is a major sign as it tells us, the observer, that something is wrong.

Other passive signs, such as constant pains and aches, are not visible, felt, or easily noticed by an observer. But a person becoming socially awkward or distancing themselves from others can be picked out from the crowd.

Hostility Toward Family and Friends

Another prominent sign that can be easily picked up is the person becoming aggressive. They would start yelling or even fighting over petty things and generally being annoying or feeling annoyed over the most insignificant things.

This type of behavior is common against friends and family. This is because the said person is the closest to them, hence why they occasionally lash out at them.

The person going through troubled times feels that their friends and family are the closest to them. So when even these groups can't understand them, they feel frustrated and take out their frustration in the form of anger.

Getting Into Drugs

A person with a mental illness cannot cope with the stress and hardships they face. They want to seek refuge from the world of problems they find themselves in, escape reality, leave their troubles behind, and be 'happy.'

So, they turn to drugs or start binge drinking alcohol. They do this to escape from all their troubles because these means of escapism give them wings to fly and leave the world behind. As they try these for the first time, they realize they can temporarily separate themselves from their troubles. The numbness they receive from drugs helps them forget. However, soon, the effects wear off, and reality hits the fan. They then continue on this path to strive for that initial feeling. Eventually, becoming addicted to the drugs, and at that point, their need to indulge in substances takes over, and it is no longer just recreational.

Body aches

People suffering from depression, stress, and anxiety tend to feel random body pain, start hearing voices, and have headaches.

These symptoms are a side effect of stress. The mind controls our body and all our voluntary or involuntary actions. So as we work our brains tirelessly by overthinking stuff, our minds are overworked and start to exhibit these pains in response.

These pains seem to be random, caused by unknown circumstances. However, these are signs of a person suffering from depression or anxiety.

A person who has a mental illness can also feel helpless. This is because they start to think that their problems keep piling up. They hadn't dealt with the previous issues when new ones came into play. All of this piling up makes the person feel helpless, not able to keep up. They realize that most people do not support them or, even if they do, can't help them solve their problems.

Suicidal Thoughts

As we feel helpless and realize that nobody cares for us or doesn't want to help us, we feel alone, lonely, and worthless. There doesn't seem to be any point in continuing our life. As life keeps going downhill and shows no improvement, we think of ending things.

For someone struggling, often suicide is the only 'logical' way to do things. In certain cases, they might even self-harm. They lose their self-worth and feel like a burden to the world. In some cases, it can also create feelings of hostility; if the world doesn't care about them, it is better to leave it behind.

Sleep Issues and Lethargy

People who suffer from mental health problems feel tired a lot. This is because they constantly ruminate on their problems. The stress their experience can be so bad that it makes it difficult for them to sleep. Even when they do, it is not restful, and they often wake up feeling tired.

Usually, this habit affects their health so much that they experience headaches or body pains. In addition, these issues with their sleep cycle further worsen their mental stability. This low energy also makes it difficult for them to work or complete other tasks. All of this only adds to the already never-ending stress they are facing.

Anger and Its Issues

When a person is already frustrated with life, they can experience anger at everything. For them, the trigger for their outbursts can be the most basic things, such as financial issues, problems relating to family, and stress. All of these can cause frustration and anger in a person.

What Is It?

Anger is a strong emotion that is caused by a lot of things. Anything can instigate someone's anger. A person who may feel joy from something can later be triggered and angered by the very same thing.

How to Control it?

Managing your anger is key to having a healthy life. This is important because when a person is angry, they usually do not make sound decisions. Also, if left unchecked, anger can take a toll on your health.

So, a person needs to keep this emotion in check.

One can manage their anger by;

Exercising

It helps release the built-up stress and frustration.

Avoiding the blame game

Find possible solutions to problems instead of shifting the blame on others.

Taking a break to calm down

Try to address the situation once you have calmed down. After which, you can express your thoughts in an assertive but nonconfrontational way.

Taking a time-out

I've learned to take 7 seconds before speaking to ensure I don't say something I might regret later.

These steps help you control your anger.

Remember, the goal here isn't to eradicate anger; it is a part of you and is helpful sometimes. You have to learn to control your anger and limit its effects.

Uncontrolled Anger

Anger is a powerful emotion. It has benefits, and it is sometimes needed. However, it can have physical and psychological side effects. Anger, if left unchecked, can grow into a monster that might destroy your life, mental health, and other social bonds. If someone suffers from uncontrollable rage, they have a high risk of becoming mentally unstable. For example, a person may start to feel angry regularly and potentially develop an anger-based personality. As a result, these individuals are more likely to have developmental problems and be mentally unstable.

Such mental instability is commonly known as 'Intermittent Explosive Disorder' or 'IED.' In an IED, a person has a habit of constantly going off in a rage of anger for no reason. One moment they would be fine, and the next, they become angry for seemingly no reason. This can be toxic and hard for others to deal with, mostly because the person is always angry.

Communication and Rationalization

Communication is something that we do in our daily lives. It is the act of interacting with someone—verbally, through body language, and written communication (like our communication through this book.). At the same time, rationalization is the act of justifying the actions you communicate, either verbally, through body language, or through communication

Why and How?

Rationalized communication is important. Communication is essential as it helps us understand the other person better. As a result, we get closer and build a friendly bond as we share our feelings and thoughts. Rationalization is also critical in a conversation as it helps a person to make logical decisions.

Striking up a conversation is easy; you just have to talk about something you have in common with the other person and build on that.

For example, you can tell the other person how you feel about the weather, and when they reply back, you can tell them how the weather affected your morning or daily routine. This would allow the other person to reply in kind, thus starting a healthy conversation. Rationalizing a conversation is essential. Rationalized communication speaks volumes of your maturity and intellect. Using it in our lives is also vital and critical for a stable mindset.

Don't be Stuck as an Introvert

Being overly introverted can also be a sign of mental stress. People are social creatures that often have circles of friends and family they rely on. Normally, we share our feelings and open up to others in intimate ways. We can keep our stress levels down by opening up and sharing our experiences. This allows us to lean on our network for support.

This support holds up our stress and insecurities. Not only that, but we also get ideas, solutions, and possible help from others. This is key to helping us move toward stability.

As we just discussed, it is powerful to get help and emotional support from others.

Kindness and Empathy

These are two sides of the same coin; one cannot exist without the other. Understanding this aspect and embracing these qualities can help make us better people.

Empathy

Empathy is the ability to understand how others feel. Therefore, it is of great importance to be emphatic to others. We saw how impactful it is when someone supports you and has your back. Understanding others around you and going the extra mile for them can bring out changes in the other person. You have to be in a good place to reciprocate while also being able to relate and give advice based on your desire to want what's best for the person and help them through their situation. Being relatable goes hand in hand with empathy, and you have to care to ignite this emotion genuinely.

Kindness

Being kind is something we learn as early as childhood. Children are taught to interact with other children and show kindness and gratitude toward one another. This is a critical part of our growth and evolvement; we support each other by being kind. It helps others to feel and experience positive reinforcement both mentally and physically.

When we care for others, they realize that they are important to us, are taken care of, and are generally not alone. Kindness, empathy, compassion, relation, and loving support are pillars for people suffering mentally or who have toxic behaviors.

All of this is needed to pull them out of their destructive cycles. In addition, helping others releases endorphins within ourselves that make us feel good, reassuring us that the good karma will be returned.

Seeing others happy due to our support gives us a sense of accomplishment that we helped them out of something detrimental to their well-being. In addition, seeing them happy enhances our mood and encourages us to do more.

"Sometimes, the best way to solve your own problems is to help someone else."

—General Iroh

CHAPTER. 7

Mental Health and Sex

"We are programmed to do so (have sex)...."

—Sex therapist, Richard A. Carroll

Sexual drive may be the most important trait for any species. On a purely biological level, it contributes to the growth and spread of a species. However, this desire varies from person to person. Sexual desire is dependent on a person's libido.

We are wired to think about sex throughout the day; the average guy thinks about it 34 times, while women think of it 19 times a day. If you add up the days and weeks, data shows that an average guy has sexual thoughts every half an hour. This isn't abnormal. Sexual desires have been with us since the beginning of time. Even the Bible mentions how Adam fell for Eve's beauty, leading him to eat the forbidden fruit when she offered it.

Sexual Desire in Nature

From a scientific perspective, sexual desires are healthy for a person. They are not weird but rather a sign of one's health. The cultural and societal stigma has taught us to discriminate against our sexual instinct. Mother Nature encourages us to copulate as much as we can.

Even in nature, you will find that different species have a life cycle that has sexual desire at the center of it. They also have the same desire. It is the most efficient way for an animal to ensure the survival of its species.

Sexual Desire in Humans

Two categories motivate a person's sexual desire. Researchers describe these as:

Body-Centered Sex

Body-centered sex focuses purely on desire, feelings, and lust. There are no emotional strings attached, nor any intimacy.

Person-Centered Sex

Person-centered sex is done to establish an emotional connection. In this type of copulation, a person's emotions play a key role, which helps enhance a relationship. They aren't driven by the need to have sex but by the need to feel intimacy with their partner.

Sexual Desire in Males

Regarding sexual desires, males tend to have a higher libido than women. Young men generally prefer body-centered sex, while females of the same age prefer person-centered sex. They also have many sexual partners in their late teens to mid-twenties. However, this begins to change as they grow older.

Sexual Desire in Females

On the other hand, females prefer person-centered sex, especially during the early years of their life. They like to have sex with someone serious and committed to the relationship.

Sex is used to initiate or strengthen a relationship. However, just like men, they, too change in the later years of their life. As they get older, they shift their sexual goals.

According to a study done by Janell Carroll and her colleagues in 1985, "*Most college-aged males preferred to have 'casual sex' rather than be in an emotional relationship.*"

However, in recent years, Janell Carroll repeated the experiment in 2006. She found, "*Instead of men and women being at opposite ends of the sexual spectrum, they are now coming together...,*" showing us how we are becoming aware as a species with time.

This is mainly because we are becoming increasingly aware of every human's fundamental rights. Equality between genders has also helped others realize equality in expressing and exploring sexual desire.

Mental Health and Sex

Mental health also plays a major role when it comes to the sexual activity of a person.

A person's sex life is affected by their mood or mental health. If someone is suffering from depression or anxiety, they may;

Have Problems In Their Sex Life

Feeling under pressure, they wouldn't be able to perform and satisfy their partner.

Suffer From Erectile Dysfunctions

Anxious people generally face problems getting aroused during sex as their worries and intrusive thoughts might overshadow the enjoyment of the act.

Have Little To No Libido

Having sex just doesn't feel appealing when so many problems loom over them.

Diversus Health has this to say; *"Depression symptoms can leave you disinterested in relationships or sex in general...."*

Accordingly, if a person has little to no mental health problems, they can enjoy sex more than their counterparts who have such issues. In addition, they want the feeling of love and care and can have a more intimate interaction with their partner than someone with mental health issues.

Intimacy and Relationships

Many people have the misconception that relationships are always intimate; however, that is not the case.

Intimacy is about the real, profound connection you and your partner create. Meaningful relationships require intimacy. As you get closer to a certain person, you start to feel emotionally connected. You love them for who they are and accept that they might change in the future.

On the other hand, a **Relationship** refers to the interaction that two people might have. This could be professional interaction between two colleagues in an office or a sexual relationship between two partners.

Intimate Relationships

Having an intimate relationship with your partner is essential. People with successful relationships generally tend to be intimate with each other. Being so close to each other, you start respecting them and develop mutual trust with your partner. You know the other person is faithful to you and would not betray your trust. In a relationship such as this, you can be vulnerable together. You and your partner are like an open book, hiding nothing from one another. As a result, you feel safe with them and can enjoy a fulfilling sex life.

Lack of Intimacy

On the other hand, a relationship that lacks intimacy cannot enjoy these kinds of luxuries. Without intimacy, you might;

Not Engage In Sexual Activities As Often

About two percent of all couples in the U.S. are married yet did not have sex for more than a year. This was the result of a case study done by the General Social Survey in 2018.

Not Feel Secure While Having Sex

Your partner feels like a stranger or someone distant from you. This makes you feel uncomfortable, and you tend to avoid having sex.

Mostly Only Do It For The Feeling Of Pleasure

Since you are not in love with the other person, the relationship starts getting linear, and a point comes where you are only in it for pleasure.

Not Enjoy Being In The Company Of The Other

Seeing them reminds you of what they might have done or whatever was the cause of the tension.

Not Care About Partner Satisfaction

At this point, you are only in it for pleasure and, therefore, do not consider your partner's feelings.

Without intimacy, a sexual relationship can quickly become toxic, affecting one's mental and physical well-being.

How Does Mental Health Affect Relationships?

Mental health problems badly affect a relationship as it burdens the partner with many responsibilities. They have to manage and support their partner and help them get through that phase. This stresses the said person, placing the onus of the burden on their partners.

Everyone may have different ways of dealing with it and have different perspectives. Mental health issues often tend to have a *'ripple effect'* on families and loved ones.

It creates tension, stress, uncertainty, and sometimes significant changes in the quality of their lives. Different family members are prone to be affected in various ways, according to what they think is best.

Being intimate with each other, a person is attached to their partner and wants the best for them regardless of the situation. When they see the person they love the most hurt before their eyes, suffering from depression, anxiety, trouble sleeping, etc., they can't help but support the person they love. As they try to help their partner, they, too, begin to suffer. This affects them in multiple ways.

Their Daily Routine

They feel tired throughout the day, exhausted from all the extra effort they have to put in for their partner.

Feeling Responsible

They might think all of it is their fault even when it isn't.

A Change In The Health Of Their Partner

It can be frustrating if your loved one's symptoms become unmanageable and their health deteriorates even further; for instance, you might have to take on more responsibilities in their place as they might not be able to do so.

Might Feel As If They Are Not Doing A Good Job

They would start going the extra mile, pushing themselves even more as they feel they are not doing 'enough.' All this can and would ultimately affect their sexual life as their partner might not feel like having sex or even develop erectile dysfunctions due to stress and anxiety.

Mental Health Issues Today

Mental health problems are becoming extremely common in today's world. Many people, married, unmarried, adults or children, suffer from mental issues or have a history of it. With the fast-paced world that we live in, more and more people suffer from anxiety and depression.

Widespread usage of social media apps such as Facebook, Instagram, Twitter, and Snapchat has also contributed to this aspect. Many people question their lives and assess their worth based on their perception of the world, as seen by their social media feeds.

Anxiety

Anxiety makes you think about all your problems, highlighting every little inconvenience to you. A person can suffer from anxiety due to;

- A problem at their workplace

- Being in a one-sided relationship

This can lead to being nervous, tense, restless, panicked, or feeling like you're in danger. These feelings lead you to overthink everything you do, hindering your ability to make any meaningful decisions. In addition, whenever you think of something, you are bombarded by an onslaught of thoughts and worries, making it difficult to concentrate.

As you sink deeper into the depths of depression, you start to feel worthless. All of this further pulls you down as you realize that you might be a burden on others.

Sex and Anxiety

Anxiety can also lead to troubles in one's sex life as it affects how one feels about their partner. A person might become disinterested in having sex because they think that they already have enough on their plate to deal with. Even if they do indulge in sexual activity with their partner, it might not go well, adding more pressure.

This type of anxiety is generally known as sexual performance anxiety. It typically occurs in men. However, in recent years there has also been a rise in the number of female patients. Both genders suffer from sexual performance anxiety.

For males, erectile dysfunction is usually the case. Men fail to get aroused during intercourse as their minds are constantly on their problems. Anxiety in females prevents them from lubricating as they fail to get aroused, resulting in complications during intercourse.

The Power Of Touch

Touch is one of the five basic senses that we possess. It is an integral part of our daily lives; without it, we cannot function. This sense is one of the main sensations that lead to arousal during sex.

Sexual Touch

The power of touch during sexual interaction is very powerful. It can change one's perspective about how they might feel about having sex. In many ways, it helps couples get closer to each other. Touching your partner during sex relieves them, heightens their pleasure, enhances intimacy, and builds emotional connection.

Touching your partner's erogenous zones might also heighten their pleasure. Understanding of sexual touch is something that people can develop with their partners over time, but people can also go to sex therapists to get help.

Non-Sexual Touch

Non-sexual physical contact is important in a relationship. While sexual touch is only valid during sex, non-sexual touch applies to every other area of our lives.

This can include basic acts such as holding hands, hugging, cuddling, leaning on each other, etc. For these, you don't even have to go to a therapist. Instead, you can initiate these with your partner from day one.

Touch is one of the most underrated senses regarding things that advance a relationship. That is why most sex therapists encourage you to seek more physical contact with your partner. They know the value that these kinds of interactions can have.

It is also important to note that while sexual pleasure is key, it is only a small part of one's relationship. Most time in a relationship is spent without having sex, so it is essential that one also focuses on this aspect of a relationship to make it more intimate and enjoyable.

Systematic Behaviors and How to Recognize Them

Mental illness is a complicated topic with many variables and components. Mental illnesses tend to stem from a central source but gradually build, worsen, or improve over time based on the actions one takes.

Additionally, people don't always realize what they feel is symptomatic of a mental illness. That's because there's an overlap with other conditions like burnout. Symptoms can start as mild as feeling low and reduced concentration. In the worst cases, it can lead to suicidal ideation, paranoia, and self-harm. Unlike in the past, today, we have so much information about the mind with so many treatment options available that it's no longer possible to ignore the signs of mental health problems around you. So, you need to be aware of the symptoms in yourself, your friends, and your family.

Understanding Mental Instability

As we grow up, we experience many phases in our lives. From our happiest moments to our saddest or ugliest ones, all of it affects the stability of our minds. Therefore, it can be said that mental instability is something that most of us have to deal with at some point in our lives.

Down the Road

When someone goes through different traumas, it can take a heavy toll on their mental health. This could even happen due to a single traumatic event, such as the passing of a loved one or our parents.

When that trauma is not processed in a healthy manner, it can lead a person to develop a mental disorder. Similarly, the quality of one's life also makes a significant difference here. People who face too many traumatic life events or have unmet basic human needs like food, a safe place, and a good support system may also develop mental health problems.

Exposure to prolonged stress and poor sleeping habits can also contribute to this.

Systematic Behaviors of Mental Instability

There are many steps and stages to a person becoming mentally unstable. Mental instability is complex, and one cannot point to one facet of a person's life – such as if a person's relationship is failing, they are mentally unstable. However, there are some signs that one can pick up by observing their behavior.

1. Prolonged or depressive sadness

2. Inability to concentrate

3. Constant over-thinking

4. Extreme mood swings

5. Lack of sleep

6. Lethargy

7. Paranoia

8. Failing relationships

Now, these are some symptoms that all of us experience at some point, but if these are so pronounced that they affect the quality of your life and make it impossible for you to go about your daily tasks, then you need to get professional help.

Remember, you cannot diagnose someone with mental illness just because they exhibit these behaviors. Only a licensed therapist or a psychiatrist is capable of diagnosing a person. Self-diagnosis is not a diagnosis. Even if you or someone around is exhibiting these symptoms, make sure to get professional help.

Sadness

This is a feeling that everyone goes through in their lives. In most cases, it stems from a sense of loss. Being a fundamental part of the human psyche, it constantly reminds us of the importance of different things. Sadness is like a dam or a wall holding the mighty river of multiple emotions at bay. Once we indulge ourselves in sorrow and open or break the barrier, all the negative emotions start to come into our minds.

While it's okay to feel sad, as no one can be upbeat every single day, there is a line that you should draw. Constantly ruminating about your loss and being unable to move on can lead you down a dark path of depression.

Dwelling in sadness or your sense of loss changes your way of thinking and understanding. It can make you more negative and ruin your optimism, making it harder for you to overcome the challenges you face in life.

Unable to Concentrate

The ability to concentrate may become diminished when a person has a mental disorder. This could be due to many reasons, such as cognitive, medical, or psychological problems, use of certain medications, or due to sleep disorders, drugs, or alcohol.

Constant Overthinking

As a person starts to overthink, they begin to question their choices. They cannot make new decisions as the fear of making the wrong choices haunts them. Even if 'the thing' didn't necessarily happen because of them, they still can't focus on a specific task. They become a slave to their thoughts, unable to escape or think for themselves.

Extreme Mood Swings

People suffering from mental health disorders might experience extreme mood swings. One moment they would be fine, working like they usually do; the next, they could lash out over the smallest of details or might suddenly feel sad.

Their mood can change at a moment's notice, making it very difficult for others to predict their behavior. It is usually triggered by stress, lack of sleep, and severe anxiety.

Lack of Sleep

A person with a mental health problem is more likely to experience insomnia This is because they stay up late overthinking their problems. Lack of sleep makes them paranoid, which, in turn, gives them problems in their daily life.

At night time, they might spend hours trying to sleep while being bombarded by their negative thoughts. This cycle starts a chain reaction. Being unable to relax or get a good night's sleep leads them to have low energy and constantly feel tired.

Lethargy

Feeling tired could lead to a person not wanting to interact with others as they lack the energy to deal with someone. As a result, they start to distance themselves from their friends and family. This harms a person's relationships and productivity as well.

In addition, it might make them more likely to go without experiencing restful sleep. In this case, even if the person sleeps for ten hours, they'll wake up feeling tired. Similarly, even doing simple tasks like cleaning the house or washing their face might feel too difficult or require too much energy.

Paranoia

A person with mental health problems could even suffer from hallucinations and paranoia. When we face adversity, our brain is constantly wired to solve problems or discover why we face these challenges. However, there are certain instances where things happen just because they can.

Life is just tough sometimes. However, it becomes harder for a person with paranoia to accept this fact. Their minds might become stuck trying to find the answer to the point where they might fabricate some things. They also constantly feel that everyone is out to get them, making it hard to distinguish between friend and foe.

They start to make up scenarios in their head and think it is true or real, even when all things say otherwise. They might accuse their partner of cheating, believe that their passed loved ones are still alive, and so on.

Failing Relationships

People with mental health problems might have poor or failing relationships, especially if the dynamic between them and their partner is dysfunctional. It should be noted that partners might support them in these troubling times and help them recover but only to a certain extent.

For those in denial of their condition, it can take them losing everything, even the bonds with their family, to finally reach out for help. As mental disorders can also kill a person's sex drive, it further harms the relationship of the affected person as they cannot satisfy their partner.

This often means that their partner might leave them.

Prevalent Mental Conditions

When it comes to mental illnesses, there are quite a few of them out there. However, some conditions are more common than others.

Anxiety Disorder

Anxiety disorder is the most common mental illness that most people suffer from worldwide. According to a study by the World Health Organization in 2015, 3.6% of the world's population suffered from anxiety In the U.S. alone, around 19.1%

of the population suffers from anxiety. Everybody, at some point in their lives, has felt anxiety. The constant overthinking about the smallest things, ranging from a presentation or a new social situation to stressing about what to wear to work or college, is usually associated with anxiety. That is normal, and most of us have these thoughts, but chronic anxiety can cause concern.

If you feel a debilitating, persistent feeling of nervousness, you may suffer from one of several common types of anxiety. Anxiety disorder is an umbrella term that consists of the following anxiety-based disorders a person can suffer from. These include;

- Generalized Anxiety Disorder (GAD)

- Panic Disorder

- Social Anxiety Disorder

- Post-Traumatic Stress Disorder (PTSD)

- Obsessive-Compulsive Disorder (OCD)

- Irrational Behaviors

Generalized Anxiety Disorder (GAD)

People who generally suffer from GAD tend to feel

1. Scared

2. Nervous

3. Anxious

The trigger for their anxiety is not linked to just one thing and could include a person's fear of meeting someone new or working on something new.

GAD's physical symptoms may include the following;

a)   Sweating

b)   Headaches

c)   Shallow breathing

d)   Heart palpitations

You might also feel nervous and scared about presenting something to your boss or a meeting but a person suffering from GAD would be apocalyptic about it, thinking and focusing on 'near-catastrophic' events happening.

They will have thoughts from both extremes, ranging from a fear of stuttering to thinking that the roof will come down or the projector will explode during the meeting. They would develop a fear of scenarios that are out of their control and are extremely unlikely to happen, but appear very real to them.

Panic Disorder

A panic attack is usually induced by a trigger that is entirely subjective. Any situation or feeling might trigger this reaction, particularly when someone feels too overwhelmed. It is something that is a natural reaction in our body.

However, if a person has these panic attacks more than two times a year, it is considered a disorder. This is because panic attacks are sudden and severe feelings of anxiety can come with many physical symptoms.

These physical symptoms could include;

- Elevated heart rate

- Sweating

- Having trouble breathing

Chest pains, similar to a heart attack.

It is important to note that most common types of anxiety come with panic attacks, but where panic disorder differs is how they occur without any other forms of day-to-day anxiety.

Social Anxiety Disorder

In this type of disorder, people are not comfortable in social settings and may avoid;

- Going to crowded places like the mall or a concert.

- Social interactions of any kind, causing them extreme anxiety, discomfort, and fear of being judged or being seen by others.

If left unchecked, in extreme cases, social anxiety can manifest into agoraphobia, where they might not want to leave the house. It is important to note that there is a difference between the introversion displayed by an introvert and a person suffering from a social anxiety disorder.

A person suffering from social anxiety disorder chooses to actively avoid people because they fear being judged, embarrassing themselves, or don't want to experience a panic attack when they are in a social setting. This fear binds them to their homes, avoiding all interactions.

This can cause their relationships to fall apart. People suffering from this disorder may also have difficulty holding permanent jobs and meeting their partners regularly.

Post-Traumatic Stress Disorder (PTSD)

As the name implies, this disorder occurs when a person goes through a traumatic event in their life and has trouble processing and moving on from that experience. After the event, the person may fear similar-looking objects or sounds similar to their traumatic event. This can cause a reaction from the patient depending on the trauma.

A well-known example was seen during World War I. After facing an intense artillery barrage, which could sometimes last for many days, soldiers were left shell-shocked. Once they were back from the war, these soldiers had a hard time integrating into civilian life as every time a loud noise was heard; these shell-shocked men would run for cover, thinking that an artillery barrage was about to commence.

As a result, they would experience the same fear and trauma when faced with an impending artillery barrage. Thankfully, with effective treatment, this is a treatable condition. Unfortunately, one does not need to be on the battlefield to experience PTSD.

There are many cases where a person has PTSD after a traumatic car accident or a life-threatening situation such as mugging or attempted murder.

Obsessive-Compulsive Disorder (OCD)

Obsessive-compulsive disorder, or OCD, is a type of mental disorder where a person can become obsessive about the importance of seemingly meaningless things in their routine. In extreme cases, they might develop a compulsion to accomplish specific daily tasks or have 'rituals' to get a particular result to calm their anxiety. A good example can be washing their hands frequently and thoroughly, fearing that they are dirty and might infect another person. A person with OCD will believe there's a particular way to wash hands or a certain number of times they must wash their hands. In such cases, they might also be driven by the fear that if they don't wash their hands like that, then something catastrophic will happen.

The compulsion can be so strong that, in some cases, a person might rub the skin raw from washing their hands frequently. Despite being in pain, they will still wash their hands because they are unable to control themselves.

Irrational Behaviors

Irrational behaviors are thoughts or actions that are not driven by logic. They are done in the 'heat of the moment.' These behaviors do not always make sense and are often not the right response to an event or a situation.

According to an experiment done in the 1970s by two Russian psychologists, humans are born irrational beings. However, as we grow up and mature, we begin to think rationally and develop reason.

Someone who thinks rationally likes to do things and handle them periodically. On the other hand, a person who doesn't 'reason' tends to do things in an unorganized manner and is generally more chaotic at work.

This type of decision-making is driven by;

- Insecure thoughts

- Emotional instability

- Anxiety

Irrational thinking can cause a person to make decisions that harm or even break relationships. According to Catherine Yeung,

"A lot of social problems are actually caused by people with irrationality."

Finding the Root Cause

Any illness or disease always has a root cause. Even natural-born diseases such as sickle cell anemia have a root cause in the parent's genes. Looking at these root causes is crucial as they help us address the real issue and create an effective treatment method.

As the old saying goes;

"Prevention is better than cure...."

—Desiderius Erasmus - Dutch philosopher

Without finding the root cause, we cannot determine what kind of cure a person would need. As we see, in the case of PTSD, trauma from something that has happened in the past causes problems in the future, and without finding what causes the trauma, we cannot deal with it. Without knowing what caused the trauma, we cannot easily determine the full extent of the sickness.

Hence, it is vital for a therapist to dig up a patient's past to get to the root cause of the problem. This would help them resolve the situation as soon as possible.

Root Causes for Mental Instability

Many things contribute to harming an individual's psyche. Most things that lead to mental instability have to do with the patient's past experiences and personality. However, personality alone cannot determine how a person will turn out, nor can a person's past determine their nature.

Instead, it is a mixture of both things. Past experiences with family and loved ones can shape us into new and different people.

Childhood

Childhood is the most important part of a person's life. A person's entire personality is shaped during their childhood. A child is like a building; if the foundations are laid strong and solid, they can handle all the storms that life throws at them. However, if the foundations aren't strong, the building will collapse as multiple storms of life hit it. Hence, a trauma or a catastrophic event during a person's childhood can build a complicated person.

Past Relationships

A relationship, be it intimate or not, shapes a person's interaction with people. In essence, it can define your interaction with other people.

We can sometimes develop trust issues when we break a relationship on bad terms. These issues can make a person less open to people around them. Past experiences play an important role in the character-building of a person. Some people find themselves betrayed by a close friend or partner, making it harder for them to open up to other people.

You might've seen people or experienced something similar yourself. For example, after your first breakup with your partner, you might have found yourself unable to trust new people easily, developing trust issues. Therefore, relationships play a significant role in developing a person's psyche.

Socio-Economic Problems

Wealth is something that has a major influence on the way a person behaves and develops mentally. You might've seen many historical examples of great men beginning their journey from rags to riches. The richest man in recorded history, John D. Rockefeller, was born into a low-income family where he and his entire family worked. He made this giant leap as he knew the value of money and worked day and night to escape their poor financial situation. In contrast, if we look at their children, we see a completely different story. Born in riches, their children do not value money as much as their parents did. Instead, they see money as something they can get at any time without much effort. That is the driving reason why children of successful people, in most cases, do not reach the same level of success as their parents.

Similarly, lack of money can be one of the driving factors which could lead to breakups and deterioration in a relationship. Couples end up fighting over money as their needs aren't being met. Once the romance dies out and they see reality for what it is, most couples start fighting as they find it hard to make ends meet.

Mental Stability and Relationships

A stable relationship requires both parties to be stable in mind and body; Being mentally stable is extremely important for a relationship to succeed. If even one person in a relationship has untreated mental issues, it would negatively impact the relationship. If you are the primary caretaker of your partner day and night, you tend to feel its effects on yourself. You could suffer from depression, anxiety, or worse, from taking care of your partner. You would need help yourself as you begin to suffer from depression.

This was a best-case scenario.

In most cases, your partner might not be as supportive. If you find yourself suffering, you could have issues over various things. These could lead to fights between you and your partner, leading to a breakup and sending you further down the depths of mental instability.

That's why it's important not to ignore signs of mental health problems in yourself or others around you. It's always a good idea to choose to see a professional who will make a significant difference in your life.

CHAPTER. 9

The Growth Process in Achieving Mental Stability and its Outcome

Achieving mental stability is a long, complex, and difficult process; you must overcome many obstacles. However, these problems only make you stronger and can help you overcome future problems too.

You can't achieve mental stability overnight; it cultivates over time. Therapy and knowing your own value can help you work toward good mental health.

The Path to Mental Stability

Before starting, it is important to know what you're looking to get out of mental stability. This helps you set targets and goals, a mental map that you can use to chart your journey.

Mental stability refers to the well-being of a person's

- Emotional

- Behavioral, and

- Cognitive abilities.

If a person is mentally strong, they can easily overcome mild symptoms of depression and anxiety. They can also build relationships and overcome different challenges in life easily.

Stages Toward Mental Stability

After deciding where you need to go, the next logical path is to find the safest and easiest route. Once you identify your illness, you must take the necessary steps to lead to your cure. There are many different routes an individual takes to reach the destination when on the road to mental stability. Some common ways you can increase your mental health and make yourself mentally stable are:

Value Yourself

You are the most valuable person in the entire world. Know that you come first and therefore have to prioritize your needs. You should go out more and find new hobbies or just make time for your hobbies. Learn to value yourself and differentiate between what is good and harmful for you.

Take Care of Your Body

Our bodies are important not just for mobility but because our physical health directly affects our mental health. So, to get a healthy mind, you need to have a healthy body as well. Some ways that you can do this are by:

Switching to a Healthy Diet

Avoid foods with too much oil or fat; instead, you should have good nutritious meals. Try to eat meals that have carbs, proteins, fiber, and more in balanced quantities.

Engage With Good-Natured People

Engage with people who are not toxic, are not always going on about themselves, and are generally helpful. Their positive energy would make you feel at home.

Have Some Alone Time

Having some *you* time is essential. Take a break from everything and everyone around you for a few hours or on weekends. During this time, do what you like, not what others tell you.

Exercise More

These could be anything, from a light walk to a full workout, but it is important that you carry out these exercises at least once a day. This would refresh your mind and give you confidence that others are willing to be in your company.

Get Enough Sleep

An average adult needs around eight to nine hours of sleep a day. A good night's sleep keeps you fresh throughout the day, enabling you to carry out multiple tasks easily.

Surround Yourself With Good People

It is important to have some alone time, but when you're around people, make sure that the people you're around are good for your mental health and well-being. Interact more with close friends, family, and relatives. The good 'vibes' that such people exude can be enough to turn your mood around. They can go a long way to improving your overall health.

Give Back to the Community

Giving back to the community can help you to feel connected to your surroundings. As you interact with others, you can feel their pain and connect to them emotionally. It teaches you to be empathetic toward others. Not only does this help you, but you also contribute to making the community better.

Learn How to Deal With Stress

Stress is a part of our lives. All of us have gone through stress at some point in life. However, we mustn't allow stress to consume us; we should manage it healthily instead of letting it become a hurdle.

Instead of always stressing about different things, we should focus on things that help us avoid stress, such as;

- Taking long nature walks

- Playing with our pets

- Writing about our problems

- Being in the company of someone we can trust, like a partner, etc.

Quieten Your Mind

There are times when your thoughts are racing, and your mind might feel like it's too loud. Such instances can worsen your overthinking and panic and make you assume things are worse than they seem.

In such instances, you need to learn to quieten your mind. You can achieve this 'emptying of the mind' by meditating and relaxing your body. This can also be achieved through prayers and supplication. Through meditation, you will be able to clear your mind, which would help in reducing stress.

Set Realistic Goals

Realistic goals generally translate into achievable goals. They're the ones where you can hammer out all the details and map out every step you need to take to get to the end result. For instance, writing what you have to do and how you'll do it will function like a plan to look at, especially when you have any doubts. A set goal also helps you prepare for financial burdens or other issues. If you don't plan for it ahead of time, you'll just end up stressing about it and failing.

Avoid Alcohol and Other Drugs

You should avoid drinking alcohol and taking drugs for recreational purposes. Even in a social setting, people use drugs and alcohol because they don't realize the harm these things can do. In truth, they do more harm to your body and ruin any progress you might have made for mental stability.

Get Help When You Need It

We usually tend to handle our problems independently. However, shouldering all the responsibility can add to your strain. Not only will it harm your mental stability, but the added stress will also cause physical health problems.

Getting help is the most efficient and helpful way of solving your problems. It's also helpful to turn toward professionals who know how to deal with your problems. As we ask others for help, we can share the burden, which greatly reduces our stress.

These points mentioned are not a cure for mental illnesses. It is always a good idea to get professional help. However, these steps can make it easier to work toward mental stability.

Importance of Mental Stability

Just like our bodies require physical exercises to remain healthy, our minds also require a stable mental state for productive and healthy thoughts.

A person with a stable mind can better deal with negative emotions and feedback. They are of more help to others, such as families and friends. Generally, they tend to have successful relationships.

A successful relationship with your partner positively affects your mental health and vice versa. This is partly because, in a successful relationship, there are lower stress levels and less depression.

Mental Stability Tools

No matter how well a person can handle stress, there are times when it gets too much. During a time such as this, a person should use some tools that help them relieve this stress. These tools are nothing but various ways to have our stress relieved and include;

Taking Slow and Deep Breaths

According to the University of Michigan Health,

"To relieve stress, the first exercise, 'below belly breathing,' is a simple to learn and easy to do exercise. It's best to start there if you have never done breathing exercises before."

Belly breathing is one of the easiest exercises to do. It helps in;

a) Relaxing the mind, and

b) Calming down a person.

This is a basic yet essential exercise that you can easily perform anywhere. It includes the following steps;

1. Lie flat or sit on the floor in a comfortable position.

2. Put one hand on your belly below your ribs and the other on your chest.

3. Take a deep breath through your nose, and let your belly push your hand out. Your chest should not move.

4. Breathe out through pursed lips as if you were whistling. Feel the hand on your belly go in, and use it to push all the air out.

5. Do this breathing exercise three to ten times. Take your time with each breath.

After exercising, notice how you feel at the end.

Soak In A Warm Bath

We need to relax our bodies every once in a while. Our mental health affects our physical health; the more stressed your body becomes, the more stressed the mind gets.

A warm bath would help in relieving this stress. To prepare such a bath;

1. Pour warm water, around 89 - 104 degrees Fahrenheit, into the bathtub.

2. Do not fill the tub all the way; instead, fill it halfway.

3. Next, pour in some pink salts.

4. Soak in that water for 10 - 20 minutes.

Listen To Soothing Music

Music helps our mind and body to relax. Different kinds of music have different effects on our bodies. According to research, *"Relaxing music can trigger the release of feel-good chemicals in the brain."*

Following this method is very easy.

1. Just put on some relaxing music

2. Sit in a comfortable chair or lie down on your bed

3. Close your eyes and just listen to the music

Practice Mindful Meditation

Mindful meditation helps a person to relieve stress and think about the present. This way, you let go of all the chaos around you. Mindful meditation allows us to focus on the present.

You can do it by trying out the following:

1. Sit with your legs crossed

2. Close your eyes and relax

3. Focus on your breathing—make it calm, not too fast or too shallow

4. Then start to focus on your surrounding noises

After that, just maintain your breathing and focus on your surroundings. Just note them in your head without changing them or being irritated by them.

Write

Writing is another way of channeling your anger and stress. This is the easiest as all you need is a pen and paper. After that, just write down your worries or thoughts on paper and express your anger and frustration with the pen.

Write down all that worries you and get to know why *"the pen is mightier than the sword."*

These were some of the best possible ways to channel your stress and anger into other things.

Mental Growth and Personality

Mental growth has a positive effect on a person's personality. As a person grows and gets closer to becoming mentally stable, their outlook on the world becomes more positive. Since they have their priorities sorted out, they can expand their horizon, look around them, and help others reach the same position.

You'll notice the following in a mentally stable person:

They don't lash out at their loved ones or friends

This goes a long way in improving the group's mood; your company is liked and wanted.

When they speak, they aren't hostile to others

They are mostly patient when dealing with others. Hence, they'll emit positive vibes that help improve the mental health of others.

Having Mental Space

This is something that everyone needs to work on. Throughout our lives, we try to do things quickly and, in doing so, fill our minds with all kinds of stuff, as we encounter multiple things on a daily basis. This hampers our ability to think and process new situations, leading to overthinking and stress.

To get out of this cycle, therapy and professional help play a crucial role for two main reasons.

Your mind is already preoccupied

If you load more things on it, it could go under and harm you instead of helping. Organizing things isn't easy to do and requires a lot of concentration and effort. Plus, there is always the chance that you do not actually know what you are doing.

A professional person knows their stuff

They know what they are dealing with and treat you accordingly. They have studied or cured many patients that suffered from similar cases. They know how to deal with your problems so that, later on in life, they don't come back to bite you.

Hence, seeking a professional in this situation would help you manage your thoughts better. It would also ensure that your past doesn't define your future.

A Supportive Relationship

In the previous chapters, we saw that if you have a partner with a mental illness and you support them, you may end up taking on their load. This also puts you in danger of being stressed and developing some mental illness of your own as a result.

Both partners should work on themselves rather than focusing on fixing the other in a relationship. This would help both people realize their own responsibilities and release that burden from their partner. When you focus on yourself, you will be able to understand your habits better. We all believe that we know ourselves the best, but the reality is that most of us really don't even know who we are.

As a society, we ignore our limits and keep working, unnecessarily burning ourselves out. Waking up means we start to pay attention to our lifestyles and set our priorities.

This positive lifestyle and mindset begin to bleed out and positively affect those closest to us. Similarly, when both partners work on themselves and improve themselves, they unconsciously improve their relationship.

This happens because after they both sort out their respective priorities, they can give more time to their partner. They feel free, not burdened by anything. Sure, they might have some stress from work or other places, but since they are mentally sound, they can process and then handle that stress.

Hence, by focusing on themselves, they improve their relationship, which further reduces any unnecessary adversities and helps them think and work through them more effectively.

PART III
3rd Dimension: Physical Wellness

CHAPTER . 10

Being Physically Active

"Honor the physical temple that houses you by eating healthfully, exercising, listening to your body's needs, and treating it with dignity and love."

— Wayne Dyer

The body is a temple in which our souls reside. It falls on us to manage this temple and not let it deteriorate. To that end, we must ensure that we give our bodies the best nutrition and are in the best physical shape through regular exercise.

Physical Exercises

Regular exercises or workouts are necessary to remain in perfect shape. Regular exercise also keeps you active, lessening the effects of the years that have been weighing you down.

There are two kinds of exercises;

1. Heavy exercises – Lifting weights to push the limits of your body.

2. Light exercises – Basic stuff, including cardio, pushups, daily walks, etc.

Both help you in keeping your body fit and healthy. However, heavy exercises are mostly for those who regularly do some kind of exercise and are slightly athletic.

On the other hand, light exercises cater more to beginners and help them stay active. Most people start with light exercises and then move on to heavy exercises. There are two main reasons for that;

First,

- Heavy exercises can be too taxing on the body and are more exhausting.

Secondly,

- If you start with heavy exercises, you are more likely to suffer from muscle damage.

Therefore, we will exclusively be looking at light exercises.

Light Exercises

Light exercises cater to all basic movements that improve our health.

"Human evolution led to five basic movements, which encompass nearly all of our everyday motions."

—Pat Davidson, Ph.D.

These basic movements include;

- Flexing at the knee

- Bending from the middle

- Tugging toward you

- Pressing away from you

- Stabilizing your core

I will tell you some light exercises to help you incorporate these movements.

You don't need to do much to start, as most of these exercises can easily be done without equipment. Just pick these and do about two sets of 12 repetitions daily either in the morning or the evening.

The exercises that would help you with all of these basic movements are;

Walks

Walking is known for the many benefits that it provides to our bodies. Walking helps us;

- Stabilize our core

- Stabilize our knees

- Remain active

- Lose excess fat

- Stabilize and improve breathing, reducing the chances of heart or lung disease

Before starting your daily walks, make sure that you are wearing good shoes. Different shoes can be used, but generally, you can use any shoe or trainers you feel comfortable with. Make sure that these shoes do not cause blisters or harm your feet. The best thing about walking is that it can easily be incorporated into our daily lives. For example, you could walk to work and back. But be sure to have some water and small snacks with you to help you replenish your energy.

If you are walking in the daytime, be sure to take your sunscreen along with a sunhat. Lastly, be sure to check the forecast and plan accordingly.

Starting Walks

Walking is the easiest exercise that we can do. Most of us walk at least one mile a day. However, it is different when we talk about walking as an exercise.

1. Straighten your back and stand in an upright position.

2. Start walking slowly and continue this for about three hundred feet.

3. After about three hundred feet, pick up the speed and start a brisk walk

4. Make sure your posture stays upright, and keep walking as far as you can.

This way, you would exercise your hip joints and your knee joints. Maintaining your posture is key, as it strengthens your core. Doing this once a day is enough to maintain a healthy body. Keep in mind that if you are new to walking as an exercise, you shouldn't over-exert yourself. If you feel you cannot walk more, do not push yourself. Rest and then try again the next day, gradually increasing your walk distance.

Running

Running is the more extreme version of the exercise and, like walking, helps strengthen your core and knee joints. Running also builds up endurance and improves breathing. For running, you do not need as much equipment as you do for walking.

All you require is a good comfortable pair of shoes. Again, make sure that you do not get blisters on your feet. And as stated before, make sure to check the forecast before starting your run. Try to manage your runs in the early mornings or the evening because running at these times is easier as the surrounding environment is much cooler than in the evenings.

Starting Runs

The most important thing to remember is that you aren't supposed to run in it, even though we call it running. Instead, you are supposed to jog slowly.

- Start by stretching your legs

- Get your posture correct

- Brisk walk for around three hundred feet

- Slowly start to jog

- Maintain your posture and jog slowly

- Always breathe in through the nose and breathe out through the mouth

Just like walking, do not over-exert yourself by running or jogging for a long period. Always bring water and stay hydrated with energizing snacks such as bananas or dates. Gradually increase your distance over time and maintain your slow speed while jogging.

Pushups

Pushups are a little bit hard for people who haven't done any kind of exercise in their lives. Pushup requires a person to use a lot of energy as it engages elbow joints, shoulders, chest muscles, back muscles, and core.

It also helps us with basic movements for a person, such as tugging toward you, pressing away from you, and stabilizing your core. Pushups can be practiced almost anywhere; you only need a mat, or you can do it directly on the ground.

There are two kinds of pushups that one can do.

One is for beginners who have not performed physical exercises before or cannot support their body weight. This is mainly because your arms are not strong enough to support the weight of your body.

The second type is the regular pushup you might've seen in ads or movies. You can directly start these if you have enough strength in your arms to lift your body.

Beginner Pushup

These pushups are designed to help develop strength in your arms and slowly move to the harder pushups. Here are the steps;

1. Put both of your knees on the ground.

2. Put your palms on the floor in their natural position, the position they would be in if you lie down.

3. Keep your palms and knees in the same position, straighten your arms, and make a sort of table in the process.

4. Now bend your elbows and go down, keeping your back straight.

5. Go down until your nose almost touches the ground.

6. After that, straighten your elbow and come back up, keeping your back straight.

7. Now repeat steps four to six.

Make sure that you do not over-exert yourself and try to increase your pushup count gradually.

Normal Pushups

These types of pushups are much more difficult compared to beginner pushups. In it, your arms have to support the weight of your entire body.

1. Put your palms and feet on the floor in their natural position, the position they would be in if you lie down.

2. After that, keeping your palms and knees in the same position, straighten your arms. Only your feet and hands should be touching the ground; everything else should be in the air.

3. Then bend your elbows and go down, keeping your back straight and ensuring that no part of your body touches the ground.

4. Go down until your nose almost touches the ground.

5. When you are done with that, straighten your elbow and come back up, keeping your back straight.

6. Repeat these steps a few times.

Stay hydrated, and do not push yourself too much. Finally, increase your pushup count over the following days to improve results.

Standing Overhead Dumbbell Presses

If running was the hard version of walking, then this is the harder version of pushups. By lifting weights over your head, you target the same muscles you would while doing pushups.

For this exercise, you either need to go to the gym or purchase light weights of up to eleven pounds. Other essential requirements include your hydration drink and some energetic snacks.

This is an example of a heavy exercise, so do not try it immediately. Instead, put some effort and time into perfecting your pushups, and then try this exercise if you are up for the challenge.

Lifting the Weights

This exercise mainly focuses on all your upper body muscles and is a good exercise that helps you tone your upper body.

1. Take 11 to 22 lbs. weights each and place them at the side of your feet.

2. After that, stand up straight.

3. Bend down, keep your back straight, and pick up the weights.

4. Then lift the weights and stand straight until you are naturally standing.

5. Correct your posture.

6. Now lift the weights over your head and hold them there for five seconds.

7. Then bring the weights down.

8. This time, lift your arms until they are perpendicular to your chest

9. Hold it for five seconds, then bring down the weights.

10. Repeat steps five to nine.

This exercise is extremely dangerous and difficult. Always hold the weights firmly when you lift them over your head. Do not over-exert yourself and put undue pressure on your body.

Exercise and Good Mood

Exercise helps us relieve stress and lower the chances of us getting ill. Doing exercises helps us;

1. Concentrate

2. Boost our mood

3. Stay aware of our surroundings

4. Improve our overall health

The mental well-being of a person is extremely important. It helps them make stable and sound decisions, as we saw in the last few chapters. Therefore, we should always go after things that give us a stable and sound mind. When we exercise,

1. The brain releases hormones that trigger a feeling of happiness and boost confidence. This, in turn,

- Improves our mood

- Helps us feel better

- Reduces anxiety and the feeling of depression

- Relieves stress

- Helps in nerve cell growth

- Increases brain activity, making one more active and energetic

2. Our blood flow increases. This is crucial because,

- Our blood carries oxygen to all the muscles

- Muscles use oxygen from the blood to make energy and function properly

- More muscle used (especially while exercising) equals more oxygen required

- As a result, our heartbeat gets faster whenever we exercise, helping pump more blood throughout the body.

All of this helps us improve our blood flow, as when exercise is over, the brain sends a signal to the body to create more red blood cells. The more red blood cells in our blood, the more oxygen they can carry and the higher our stamina.

This way, our health improves. The daily high blood pressure in the body due to exercise improves the pathway of the blood, resulting in a more efficient blood flow than before.

Benefits of Regular Exercising

When you start to exercise, you burn a lot of carbs and fats. All of this useless fat being burnt daily helps you control your weight. Since you have less fat all over the body, it reduces the chances of a heart attack or other heart disease.

In addition, your insulin and blood sugar levels are kept in check as your body constantly burns fats and other sugars. Constant exercises also help you to quit smoking or avoid drinking. You begin to value yourself and realize that smoking is detrimental to your health and can kill you.

As I mentioned above, exercising also helps you improve your mental health. It develops concentration and refines the ability to think critically.

These help you in moving forward and make life easier for you.

"When you exercise, your mind and body work together to build a temple for your soul."

—**The unknown soldier**

CHAPTER . 11

A Healthy Diet

A well-balanced diet is one of the most important requirements for a healthy life. Even exercising won't help you if you are not eating properly. If you mostly eat organic food, your body will remain healthy. On the other hand, if you consume junk food most of the time, then over time, your health will start to decline. In short, the better you eat, the better you will feel, and vice versa. Then, it goes without saying that unhealthy diets are not good for our bodies.

What Counts as a Healthy Diet?

A healthy diet consists of all the essential nutrients the body requires. These can vary from person to person, but everybody generally requires the same nutrients and vitamins. If you have an unhealthy diet, your body won't function properly. The best diet that meets all your nutritional needs is a varied one consisting of different healthy foods such as:

- Fruits

- Vegetables

- Nuts

- Legumes

- Wholegrain

- Meat

These foods provide essential macro and micronutrients like Omega 3 fatty acids, proteins, vitamins, and fiber. A well-balanced diet helps us maintain a strong immune system and prevents many diseases. So the healthier our diets are, the stronger and more effective our immune system becomes.

Eating healthily can also help prevent other diseases such as:

1. Obesity

2. Stroke

3. Multiple heart diseases

4. Type 2 diabetes

Eating a nutritious diet boosts your energy. It also goes a long way in improving your mood, as your diet affects you mentally, physically, and emotionally. After all, it is said,

"You are what you eat."

The Benefits of a Healthy Diet

When our body receives all the essential nutrients needed, it boosts our immunity and strengthens our bodies. Not only that, but it also performs other bodily functions such as digestion, blood circulation, and respiration without any issues. A well-balanced diet improves your life expectancy as every part of your body is maintained and functions optimally. This helps improve the body's performance and prolongs your life.

When we eat nourishing foods, we get the following benefits:

Our Muscles Get Stronger

Strong muscles facilitate better joint movement, increasing mobility and decreasing mobility problems in old age.

Our Bones Get Stronger

The stronger your bones, the stronger your teeth and bones become, and your body can handle physical stress. Having stronger bones also mean a lower chance of breaking or fracturing.

Healthy Skin

Your skin is the largest external organ of your body, and a healthy diet can improve and enhance your skin. Certain antioxidants in our diet also protect our skin from harmful free radicals, UV rays, and pollutants like smoke and other chemicals.

Your diet can improve skin health, boost collagen production and give you a more youthful appearance.

A Healthy Mind and Body

We are always told how a good diet makes a difference in our physical health. But there is another aspect which is improved by having a good diet - our mental health.

The following are some ways that a healthy diet improves our mental health and sense of well-being.

Balancing Out Hormones

Our body starts functioning at a nutritional deficit when we eat an unhealthy diet. In addition, lacking certain vitamins and minerals can cause issues with the thyroid gland and the body's endocrine system, ruining hormone production. A hormonal imbalance can leave one at risk of getting depression and anxiety. And when depressed, most of us tend to reach for processed foods, which only worsens our anxiety.

The Mind and the Digestive System

We should be mindful of what and how much we eat. Even overeating something healthy can be harmful. Too much of a good thing can be bad for you. It is interesting to note that our mind is also connected to our digestive system.

Even scientists believe this. Researchers have even found a nerve that links the brain and gut together. The American Psychologist Association stated that;

"Gut bacteria produces an array of neurochemicals that the brain uses for the regulation of physiological and mental processes, including mood. It's believed that 95 percent of the body's supply of serotonin, a mood stabilizer, is produced by gut bacteria. Stress is thought to suppress beneficial gut bacteria."

This means that helpful bacteria in the gut produce hormones that directly affect our mood. However, this bacterium gets suppressed when we are depressed or sad. Therefore, we should eat healthily for the sake of our mental health too.

Improved Immune System

Our immune system plays an important role in the body. Without its help, the body cannot fight off any disease, no matter how dangerous it may be. That is why people with weak immune systems must always care for themselves because their immune systems cannot fight back.

The immune system is built mainly on two types of white blood cells;

Phagocytes

Phagocytes go to the infectious site and envelop or eat the foreign body. Unfortunately, this method isn't always effective as some foreign bodies can overwhelm the phagocytes. After this, the body mostly relies on lymphocytes to defeat the foreign body.

Lymphocytes.

Once the body identifies a foreign particle, it produces antibodies to destroy and fight it. Lymphocytes keep on making new antibodies to defeat the foreign body. When the threat has been dealt with, the lymphocyte stores the information of the specific antibody which defeated that foreign body. This information is then later used when a similar foreign body attacks. This is how vaccines also work. To produce this army of phagocytes and lymphocytes, the body needs a lot of nutrients to survive. Therefore, they depend completely on the availability of nutrients through which they can rapidly multiply. That is why we need a balanced diet so that our bodies can maintain their immune response.

Macronutrients

Macronutrients are an important part of our diet. Hence the reason why the body requires them in large numbers. These nutrients are not small enough to be directly used by individual cells. Instead, they are found in the blood and are broken down into smaller nutrients to be used by the cells. Macronutrients generally consist of carbohydrates, proteins, and fats.

These are essential for the body as they can easily be broken down and used at any moment.

According to WHO:

"Macronutrients are nutrients that provide calories or energy and are required in large amounts to maintain body functions and carry out the activities of daily life. There are three broad classes of macronutrients: proteins, carbohydrates, and fats."

All carbohydrates are eventually broken down into simpler molecules. For example, proteins are broken down into amines, carbohydrates are broken down into glucose, and fats are broken down into lipids.

All of this breaking down is done with the help of different specific enzymes. Every macromolecule is eventually turned into glucose. This is done because our bodies cannot handle complex sugars like fructose and need it to be broken down into the simplest available form; glucose.

This glucose is then used in the Krebs cycle, where glucose is used to make an element called ATP or Adino Tri Phosphate. ATP is then used throughout the body as a packet of energy.

Whenever the body needs energy, ATP is there to provide it and help the body perform its function. Even the simplest functions, like our hearts beating or muscle's movements, require ATP. This is why macronutrients are so essential for the body.

Keeping Macronutrients in Check

Although macronutrients are very beneficial for the body, an excess could lead to problems. Macronutrients are always present in the blood, and although it is rare for micronutrients to accumulate in the blood in large quantities, it is not impossible.

Excess amounts of macronutrients in the blood can lead to other diseases, so we need to keep these levels in check. The most efficient way is to keep checking these levels. There are different ways you can check your daily intake of micronutrients:

1. First, you need to determine how many calories there are in your food and how many of them you take.

2. Then you need to determine the average amount of calories you can intake. This can be done by finding out the percentage of proteins, carbohydrates, and fats in your intake. For example, an ideal amount could be 50% carbs, 25% fat, and 25% protein.

3. Then, multiply your daily intake of calories by the percentages.

4. After that, divide your calorie number by its respective calorie-per-gram.

This way, you yourself can measure your daily calorie intake.

If all of this sounds too complicated, then you can just track them on an app. Some free apps that you can use are *Cronometer, FoodNoms, and MyFitnessPal.* These can help you in tracking your daily calories.

Relationships and Their Effects on Our Bodies and How Our Bodies Affect Our Relationship

Relationships directly affect the well-being of our minds; for instance, a good and healthy relationship can help cure depression, anxiety, and other mental disorders. However, that's not the only thing affected by relationships, as relationships also affect our bodies.

Our minds and bodies are connected, so when we are stressed, our bodies are stressed. Conversely, when we are happy, we become more energetic and playful. This happens because of our mental state's effects on our bodies.

Self-Satisfaction and Confidence Boost

Many things in life give us a confidence boost. It could be getting good grades, a promotion, some encouragement, knowledge, or anything that can boost your confidence as long as it gives you some sense of self-satisfaction. So, let's start by discussing self-satisfaction and how it can boost our confidence.

Self-Satisfaction

Self-satisfaction is the satisfaction you get when you achieve something and feel a sense of happiness.

Most of the time, this happiness isn't everlasting and only makes you happy at that moment. For example, you buy a pizza, an expensive watch, or the latest iPhone, but the happiness you get from these items would be short-lived.

As long as you eat that pizza, you will feel happy; you might crave more after it is finished or be satisfied with what you had. Similarly, as long as you have the latest iPhone model, you will be satisfied and happy, but come September, when your iPhone gets old, you will desire the newer model.

So, in essence, self-satisfaction targets;

1. One's self

2. Desires

3. Thoughts

It is different for everyone. Based on our experiences throughout our lives, we derive joy and satisfaction from different things, even relationships. Some people want a satisfying relationship and make small goals in that relationship. When those goals are realized, a sense of satisfaction is achieved because you know your relationship is going well. In addition, you realize that you are just a cog in the grand scheme.

This reminds me of a quote said by Sir Arthur;

"Lives are meaningless when you look at the bigger picture, but once you shrink down at the individual level; there is nothing more precious than a single life."

Confidence From Self-Satisfaction

We get a little confidence boost when we achieve something in life. You know your effort wasn't for nothing when your hard work pays off and you get a sense of satisfaction which translates into a boost in confidence.

When you know that everything is going according to plan, you feel a sense of relief. Satisfying our needs brings us closer to being happy and confident in life. When our life seems 'satisfying,' we automatically gain some confidence. This mainly comes as we realize that whatever we have done has brought us a satisfying life.

There is also a flip side to it.

If you indulge in too many self-serving things, your needs increase. At one point, buying a new mobile becomes a necessity rather than a need. And if you cannot satisfy that necessity, you fall into the pit of self-doubt. Gaining too much confidence can make us arrogant, and we tend to make foolish mistakes in our arrogance. That is why in life, everything is subjective. Some things bring happiness to some people, while the same things are just a norm for some people. Even the debate about whether money brings happiness or family brings happiness is subjective.

The one with a family doesn't know its value, and the one with money doesn't know its value.

Harmful Body Care Mechanisms in Relationships

In life, different individuals face different problems. Every person goes through some trauma in life. Some try to suppress it, while others try to divert their mind from the problem by indulging in different things. This is known as a coping mechanism and is harmful to the body and mind. Coping mechanisms are ways individuals bury their troubles and try to avoid them as much as possible. This is done by distracting your mind to different things like;

- Sleeping too much

- Stress eating or undereating

- Excessive alcohol

- Drug use

- Impulsive behavior

- Avoiding issues

Most individuals use one or the other kind of coping mechanism to get away from their problem. Some even use multiple coping mechanisms to escape their problems and live happy lives. People who use coping mechanisms are more likely to suffer from issues like;

- Late-life depression

- Anxiety

- Self-doubt

All of this leads to further life problems, which can devastate a person.

Coping mechanisms are mainly used because many think they can avoid the problem just by burying their heads under the sand, like an ostrich. This, however, is not true, as just avoiding the problem won't make it go away. If you avoid them or use other means like drugs or alcohol to distract yourself, you'll only make things worse.

Over and Under Eating

Our stomachs begin to expand when we eat more than the normal amount. When our stomach expands, it pushes against other surrounding organs. As the organs get compressed by the ever-expanding stomach, you feel uncomfortable. The brain reacts to the situation by slowing down your movements and making you feel lethargic. This, then, affects your work and relationships negatively. You feel too tired to do anything productive, adding to your list of problems. Similarly, you will feel lethargic if you do not eat or restrict your diet, resulting in less energy because of the small amounts of food intake. This then has the same social effect as overeating would have.

When stressed, people tend to eat without focusing on how much they eat. Eating too much can lead to obesity, which triggers a list of diseases related to the heart. When you become obese, you become conscious of your weight and stress about what people might think when they see you. Some people even lose their motivation to achieve things by doubting their capabilities.

This pushes them further down the pits of depression and disparity.

Hiding From Your Problems

Another method that some people use to get away from their problems is avoiding their problems altogether or using drugs. Anxious avoidance is a common tactic many people employ, as it makes sense to avoid things that might be harmful to you.

However, this isn't how things work, as sometimes it is better to face the problem than avoid it. If you face something, you become accustomed to it and lose fear.

Alcohol and Drugs

Drinking or using drugs is probably the most common way many people avoid certain problems. Sure, using drugs helps you a lot in numbing your feelings and suppressing your emotions, but the cons outweigh the pros.

An overdose of drugs can lead to serious health problems and even death. Drugs are highly addictive, so it is extremely difficult to leave them once you don't want to use them anymore. In addition, excessive drinking can cause many hepatic diseases as alcohol slowly destroys your liver.

Be Positive

To avoid all this, you should develop a positive coping mechanism. Learn to face your problems rather than run away from them. This helps you quickly solve the problem or make the necessary adjustments rather than *'saving the problem for another day.'*

Life won't stop throwing problems at you because you avoid certain issues. You will just be bombarded with more problems which will eventually break you. So, it is better to face your problems than just piling them up one after the other.

Lack of Social Relationships and Physical Health

Relationships come in many forms, and we as humans have been tuned in a way that we crave relationships. Probably due to the realization during our times in caves that strength is in numbers, we have begun to cherish and develop these bonds.

However, this is a general rule and doesn't apply equally to every person. For example, many people enjoy solitude more than being with others.

Solitude isn't a bad thing if one desires it, and like everything, it comes with its drawbacks and benefits. Being alone can give you time to:

- Meditate

- Read and learn

- Organize your thoughts

- Strategize and prioritize life

- Refresh your mind

Unfortunately, too much solitude can be harmful to your mental health. We have already discussed how being overly introverted can lead to the following:

- Depression

- Anxiety

- Stress from overthinking

- Feelings of loneliness

These issues open up a pandora's box and unleash other problems such as;

- Obesity

- Inflammation

- High blood pressure

Further leading to long-term health issues that can also include;

- Heart disease

- Stroke

- Cancer

Distancing yourself from other relationships is not exactly being an introvert, but at the same time, it can have similar effects on the mind and body. Social relationships refer to relationships between parents, friends, or spouses.

People usually distance themselves from these relationships because of familial problems, traumatic event(s), or the loss of trust.

All of this isn't healthy for the mind and leads to stress as you overthink your situation. This could lead to you sleeping too much, stress eating or undereating, excessive use of alcohol, drug use, impulsive sleeping, and avoiding issues. These problems would also affect your other relationships and stress your loved ones. For example, if you have a partner, they would get stressed, seeing your physical and mental health deteriorate.

If you get diagnosed with some disease, your partner will have to care for you. They will need to make sure that you don't do something irrational like eating unnecessarily, skipping exercises, and mixing medications. This would put unnecessary stress on them as they would have to look after your needs.

It is not like they can just give up on you and leave you in your state. They care for you, love you, and would not leave you in your hour of need. However, this won't be fair to them as they would have to deal with something that isn't actually their problem.

Benefits of Physical Health in Relationships

There are many benefits of having a good and healthy body. For example, we have discussed how having a good physical body can help you avoid certain psychological and physical diseases. Another benefit of having a good body is that it allows you to have a positive relationship with your partner.

When you develop your body, you become more energetic and more active. All of this translates into your sex life. When you work out, you generally become more attractive. Throughout the process of human evolution, our minds have been trained to see comfort in the arms of a powerful partner.

That way of looking at your partner hasn't changed, be it male or female; exercising makes us look sexier in the eyes of our partner.

As Dr. Penhollow explains, *"Being active leads to a more positive body image..."*

Not only this but exercising also improves your confidence and sexual performance. This is helped by your good-shaped body, which makes you capable of having prolonged intimate relations with your partner.

As your sexual performance in bed increases and you can satisfy your partner, you become more confident. This also goes a long way in improving your relationship as you become more open and closer to your partner. When you are confident, you are not afraid to share personal things with your partner.

Physical exercise also helps women be more easily turned on in bed. This is partly due to the increased blood flow caused by frequent exercise. An increase in blood flow is helpful for both men and women as it helps them in arousal during sex, leading to better sex life.

Doing regular exercise also helps in relieving stress and improves your mood. Having a lot of stress can decrease libido, leading to a deterioration in the relationship. In addition, we release certain hormones that help us improve our mood when we exercise. A positive mood can increase your libido and can help you develop a better relationship with your partner.

Having a healthy body will also motivate your partner to work on themselves. Therefore, they would be motivated to go with you to exercise. Exercising together helps you strengthen your emotional bond. When you exercise together, you and your partner become in sync.

Relationships are built on shared experiences. All our life partnerships are based on a sense of mutual understanding and common things that connect us. As we grow closer to one another, we find more things that we have in common and come to respect things that aren't.

Hence, doing familiar things helps you in improving your relationships. It adds discipline to your life and relationship as you begin to synchronize with each other.

When you work out with a partner, you get someone who will constantly motivate you to go to the gym or out for jogs in the park. If you feel lazy and tired, your partner will drag you out of bed and take you with them for the training. Not only this, but you also get encouragement from that said partner as they might challenge you to some competition. This will help you improve your routine and get ahead in your game. It's one great reason why having a partner for exercise is important. It will give your relationship a short boost and will lead to a healthy and long relationship.

CHAPTER . 13

The Outcome of Feeling Good On the Inside

A healthy body is touted as something desirable. For example, we are told that if we can get the perfect body, we will become more active and successful in our relationships. But we are never told what exactly is a healthy body. We have defined stereotypical perceptions of bodies for men, especially women, indirectly forcing them to adopt these 'healthy' bodies. Unfortunately, these can actually be harmful to your health and could leave long-term negative effects.

True Health

We have already seen the methods to get a healthy body. These include having a well-balanced and nutritious diet along with regular exercise. But what does it mean to be truly healthy? Many characteristics define what a healthy body should look like. All of these can be used to judge whether your body is healthy or not. Another thing that you should note is that not everyone has the same idea about what a healthy body is. Everyone has a different body and a different mind. What works for others won't necessarily work for you. When you exercise regularly and maintain a balanced diet, some of the signs of improvement that the body shows are,

- Improved flexibility

- Healthy body weight

- Clear eyes

- Fewer chances of getting ill

- Improved bowel movements

- Better emotional healthy

- Flawless skin

However, the first sign your body shows after exercising is that you become more flexible. You can get up easily, and your overall movements will become much easier.

When we exercise, we use our muscles regularly, improving their overall lifespan. Our body is very efficient when it comes to maintaining itself. Any part of the body that is not in regular use will weaken. That is one reason your muscles deteriorate after not exercising for a few weeks. Frequent exercise can help maintain a healthy weight for overweight or underweight people. However, when you start exercising, your instructors first tell you to change your diet. If you are skinny, you are told to increase the protein content in your diet. If you are obese or overweight, you are told to reduce your diet accordingly. This way, you get the most benefit from your exercise. Another sign of your body's growing health is that you don't easily get ill. Your body's immune system develops and can grow stronger when you eat a nutritious diet and consistently work out. This helps your immune system easily fight diseases, preventing you from getting ill frequently. Another benefit of a healthy diet and avoiding oily foods is that it can help with your bowel movements. This is mainly because of the reduction in certain toxins that helps your digestive system work properly.

In addition, a nutritional diet can also improve your skin and dark circles around the eyes. Your physical appearance isn't the only thing that changes when you go to the gym. Your mental health is also affected positively and improves. For example, you are less prone to suffer from depression or anxiety if you regularly exercise. This is because frequent exercise helps your body to circulate and release certain toxins, which help in improving your overall mood.

False Health

When describing what is considered a healthy body and what isn't, society mostly tends to provide its own version. When we think of the 'ideal' female body, most of us think of one of two things – a thin yet athletic body akin to a supermodel or a highly curvaceous body. Both are seen as the definition of a physically fit body. Similarly, for men, we think that being healthy is all about being super bulky or skinny. The truth cannot be further from this.

Many men and women with super voluptuous or muscular bodies can get that way after being on medication or having surgeries. These medications usually have side effects that show years later. A few among the sea of side effects are,

- Hair damage

- Patches on skins

- Random body pains

On the other hand, a skinny body is also usually acquired after taking medications and frequently starving yourself. Both of them are unhealthy and can have long-term negative effects. These also negatively affect your mental health, leading to self-doubt, depression, and anxiety.

Your relationship can also be affected as you cannot maintain that 'perfect' body for a long time, and eventually, your body will give up.

This might negatively affect the relationship as your partner might not find you as attractive as before or vice versa. Therefore, you should exercise according to your BMI. Every individual has their own bodily requirements depending on their height and age. We should all work toward that rather than obsessing about becoming too muscular or skinny.

Good From the Inside

We should strive toward feeling good from the inside. The simplest reason is that our bodies are like temples and must be taken care of.

We discussed this issue in the previous chapters and how we need to maintain outward appearance since our bodies are temples for our souls. Unlike our outer body, exercising cannot fix our inner form. We need to try different avenues to improve our mental health.

Feeling good from the inside is important because your soul is you; when it feels good, you will feel good. With a healthy mind, you;

- Are better connected with yourself

- Have the chance to clear your mind

- Are able to get your priorities straight

- Can better understand the society around you

- Build empathy and compassion for others

When we know how the other person feels, we start to consider their feelings and sometimes also try to help them with their problems. However, if someone has too many problems and doesn't even have themselves figured out, most people tend to avoid them. That is one of the reasons why we should also present ourselves as a whole, both in mind and body. We want others to be compatible and uncomplicated with us. Similarly, we should not complicate ourselves and expect people to want to be with us.

Historically speaking, humans have always opted for the best and easiest ways to do things. Trade, wars, work, life, and interaction with others are only preferred when they are unchallenging. Sure, a select few people would stick by you no matter how complex you are, but most of us are not like that. We prefer to meet someone we can easily understand and have a good time with. That is one of the main reasons most relationships are based on common things found between the partners. People tend to like others with a similar nature rather than someone covered in many complicated layers. That is why we should present ourselves as whole and healthy human beings.

Mind, Body and Relationships

There are a lot of benefits that one gets from having a healthy body. A healthy body influences many of your decisions in life and helps you achieve many things. We just covered how having a healthy body can lead to better health and a better mind. So, let's further discuss how a healthy body affects the mind. A healthy body means that you have a better immune system and do not easily fall ill. When you are ill, you tend to feel depressed and down. You don't feel like doing anything at all, and even if you do, you are 'chained' to your bed by the doctor. Add all this to being alone most of the day, and all kinds of worries and depression will play out in your life.

When we are sick, we often have a lot of free time to think. And many of those thoughts are worries over sickness. This, along with having no energy to fight these thoughts, will have you fall further ill or start feeling depressed. This state of mind tends to persist even after you have recovered, keeping you in the pool of depression and anxiety.

Apart from this, you are more likely to have bad skin and other skin-related issues. This leads to problems like self-doubt and many complexes, leaving you in a cranky mood and conscious of yourself. In a worst-case scenario, it can also lead to self-isolation, causing a person to become more introverted.

Having a healthy body keeps you away from these problems. Giving a boost to your immune system prevents you from falling ill. It also prevents certain skin diseases as your body can maintain the skin better.

All of this has a tremendous effect on our relationship. If you have a healthy body and mind, you can better understand your partner and support them in trying times. Remember, when you're well and healthy, your partner is also motivated to maintain a healthy body. This opens up a new chapter in the book of your relationship. On the flip side, you can have many physical and mental health problems if you do not care for yourself. This would then put pressure on your partner and would test the relationship. If your partner decides to stick with you, your problems will also affect their mental health. This could, after some time, introduce toxicity in the relationship, or it will fall apart, leaving you with further chaos and mental issues.

These are a few reasons why it is necessary to have a healthy body. Even if you aren't in a relationship right now, you will be with someone in the future, at which point you will find it difficult to start the whole process from scratch. Having a healthy body also gives you some personal time to help you reflect upon yourself and plan your life. You also start feeling more comfortable in your own skin, which boosts your confidence and makes you a more friendly and open person Even people around you begin to notice the 'changed' you, and since you are more open, they can easily approach you and talk to you. You do not make them feel uneasy or uncomfortable. Rather, you become a person in whose presence people want to be most of the time.

PART IV
4th Dimension: Spiritual Wellness

CHAPTER. 14

The Domains of Spirituality

"Spirituality is not adopting more beliefs and assumptions but uncovering the best in you."

— Amit Ray

Your true self is always within you; no matter how young or old you get, your true nature does not change. However, over the years, our true selves keep getting buried under a pile of emotions, beliefs, and societal norms. In order to uncover your original form, you must pull apart the layers you have built throughout the years.

You can find your true spiritual self and discover more about yourself in the process. This will help you explore new avenues of life that you never even thought of.

Spirituality

Spirituality stems from the place within you where you find inner peace. It is where you can easily be yourself without any worries, free from distractions, and having the ability to manage your thoughts and achieve stability in life. We have talked about why it is important to manage our thoughts and get them in order and how this helps us clear our minds and get our priorities right.

Spirituality is similar; it is a journey where you look for, and try to find your true self. After finding your spiritual self, you realize that life isn't just about waking up in the morning, doing your daily routines, and then going to bed at the end of the day.

Instead, you open your mind to other possibilities and look at things outside your daily routine that have always been within your reach but invisible. You realize that you are a part of something bigger.

By embracing this realization, you open your heart to the many possibilities that surround you but have been overshadowed by your ego, which blinds you to all the opportunities and potential.

Your purpose isn't just to become a 'slave' to society. Rather, it is to create a life that benefits you and others around you. After you open your mind and reach your inner self, you can affirm your ego and let all the positive emotions flow. You will experience an increased capacity for;

Love – You feel a deep connection to people and nature, which develops from having a better understanding of yourself.

Generosity – Once you begin to feel connected to the knowing of a higher purpose in life, you realize that most material things are of little value. You understand that no life is greater than another, and everyone deserves an equal chance, prompting you to help those less fortunate than you.

Self-Worth – You become aware of your limits by becoming mindful of your strengths and weaknesses. You develop the power to say 'no' if someone asks you to do things against your beliefs. You validate and honor your beliefs and you defend your inner child because of the tremendous love you have for yourself.

Self-Esteem – You become more confident in your own skin and honor who you have grown and evolved to be. Each one of us has a unique gift to offer this world, and once we realize what is ours, we will own it and be proud of what we contribute to society.

Spiritual Health

Spiritual care consists of things that are more than just daily pushups or a visit to the gym. You instead reach it through things like meditation and balancing your chakra system.

Chakras allow you to balance your emotions which gives you a sense of security and growth, among other things. They also help you in feeling positive and optimistic. Your chakra system allows your energetic system to breathe—just as you have a muscular system, a nervous system, a skeletal system, and so on. Keeping your chakra system healthy so the energy passes through and does not stay stagnant is important and done so through meditation and healthy life habits.

Overall, spirituality allows you to look at the bigger picture. It allows you to feel empathy and look at the world from another perspective. Looking at the 'bigger picture' allows you to see life's complexities, providing you with a different perspective.

You realize that failure is a part of life and do not have to run from it. This helps boost your confidence and find different, if not multiple, reasons to enjoy life. You find joy in the simplest of things in life. You'll see the joy of walking in the park or sitting on the couch with your significant other. You'll feel happy and filled with positive energy. This energy flow will also help the organs, body, and mind work at their best capacity. You will also see improvement in your mood, muscle movement, and digestion. All of this helps you connect the inner world with the outer one. You do not have to focus on these two separately or focus on one and leave the other. Instead, you can find balance in the many connections found between nature.

"The greatest illusion of this world is the illusion of separation. Things you think are separate and different are actually one and the same."

— **Guru Pathik**

Moving Toward Spirituality

Spiritual awakening can be triggered by anything. Sometimes, it is done consciously through meditation and concentration. Other times it gets triggered unconsciously. It can be a small thing or a major event that could change the whole outlook on your life. Many signs and life changes indicate that you are about to have or are going through a spiritual awakening. Sometimes, they can be repeated events that give you a feeling of *'déjà vu'* and make you question things.

The Questioning Phase – You start feeling detached or unfamiliar with activities you previously liked or enjoyed. This is a sign that you are not content with what you have and want to find a better purpose in life, leading you to assess your beliefs and reevaluate your values and beliefs.

The Realization – Your entire overview of things changes, and new doors open in your life. You realize that everything is connected, and no one is alone.

Being Free – When your mind opens up, you see things for what they are. You start to explore the world or pursue your long-forgotten dreams. Many events in our lives seem similar; every passing day feels the same. When you get a sense of freedom, you may feel a calling or connection to nature, enhancing your senses and making you more aware of your surroundings.

Most commonly, many people feel empathy, followed by generosity. When you start seeing all these signs, you could feel lonely and distant from others as their way of life and yours no longer align.

These can be signs that you are going through a spiritual awakening. These things can be complicated to understand as every individual will have a different perspective on different events. But everything becomes clear as the signs continue to unfold and you are placed on your soul path.

Your Chakra System

Chakra meaning 'Wheel' in Sanskrit, is energy that flows throughout our bodies. There are seven main chakra points, but more that flow throughout our bodies. These seven main chakra points start from the bottom of our spine and go up to our heads.

All of these chakra points are energy gates that are found throughout the body. These energy gates or points allow energy to flow through the body, thus spinning the chakra centers. When energy flows freely throughout our body, spirit, and mind, all are positively affected. Therefore, if we want to allow our spiritual energy to flow through our body, we need to open each gate so that all energy can easily flow through the body. Energy gets blocked and stagnant with toxic thinking and environments and need to be cleared. This is done through meditation, where you connect with your inner self and help it open the different gates of the chakra. Think of these chakra gates as a water wheel; each gate carries or transfers the energy into the next one, making the entire wheel spin. However, even if one of them gets blocked, the entire wheel either slows down or stops spinning. Therefore, all seven gates are opened in order, i.e., bottom-up. Each of them has its own color, symbol, and meaning. If you do not open all your chakras, your true potential is locked and cannot be accessed.

The energy that flows through your chakras also relates to your physical outer world. When you live in this world on a higher vibration, i.e., being a moral/ ethical person with compassion and humility, this results in cleaner energy flowing throughout your body, thus keeping your mind, body, and spirit aligned and healthy.

Root Chakra

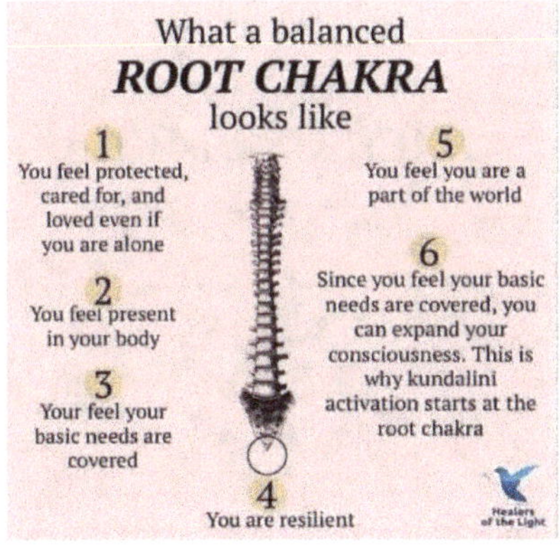

Many people think that the first chakra gate that we should open is the crown chakra. However, It is the root chakra that needs to be opened first. Denoted by the color red, the best way to open the root chakra is to let your anger flow and become accepting of your mistakes. One way to do that is to try the *Mountain and Tree* yoga poses. Doing this connects your physical energy with the Earth itself, grounding the negative energy you have. This is also the main reason we start with this particular chakra, as all our negative energy gets grounded, and we can start fresh.

When you let go of your anger and let bygones be bygones, you feel a sense of security and independence. This helps you in taking in all the love of your world. You become present in your mind and body when you release the anger. You can make decisions consciously rather than being driven by impulse.

Sacral Chakra

The second gate that you open is the sacral chakra. The color of this chakra is orange. For this gate, you need to focus on why you are frustrated and what problems make you feel like this. With practice and release of these emotions, you can control your emotional outbursts and develop a feeling of self-worth, increasing your creativity. *Revolved Triangle and Goddess* yoga poses are some of the best ways to open this gate.

This chakra helps you connect with your creative identity and helps to release most of the useless sex-obsessed thoughts. You will notice an improvement in your sex life and will become more confident about your sexuality.

Solar Plexus Chakra

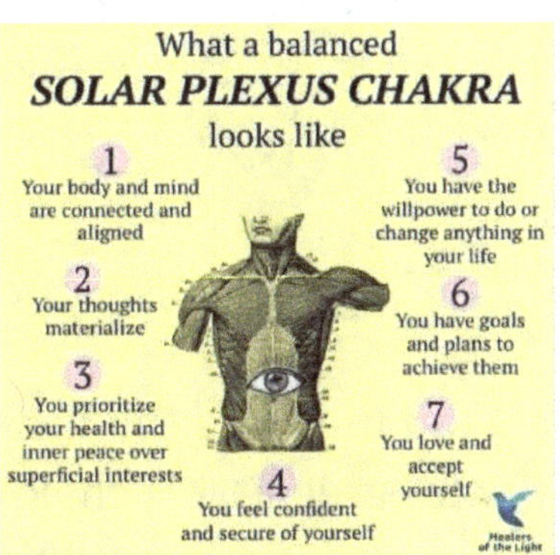

The third chakra is the solar plexus chakra, found in the stomach and is yellow in color. To unlock this gate, you must learn to control your ego and balance your aggression toward different things. When the solar plexus gate opens up, it helps your digestion as the chakra in the stomach can flow freely. You achieve these through the *Boat* and the *Downward-Facing Dog* yoga poses.

Opening this chakra gate increases your productivity, helping you achieve your life's goals and plans. Working with this chakra will also help you learn to accept yourself and love who you are. You will find an increase in willpower, making you more prone to achieving your goals.

Heart Chakra

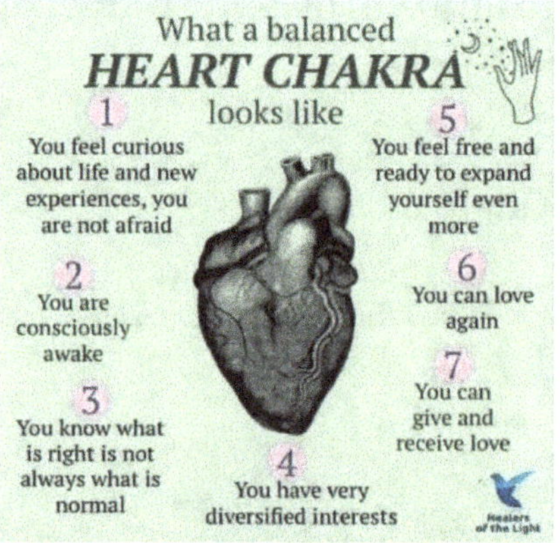

The fourth chakra in line is the heart chakra gate, signified by the color green. This chakra connects the bottom chakras, the first three, and the top chakras, the last three. If this chakra gate is blocked, one cannot move on to the next stage of enlightenment and growth. Use *Low Lunge* and *Camel* yoga poses, to open this gate along with meditations of peace, love, and connectedness to all.

The heart chakra is opened by learning to trust others, managing your moods, and accepting your fears. This then helps you become consciously awake and more aware of your surroundings. When you deal with your moods and fears, you also become curious about yourself and your life. You will develop a love for yourself that is unconditional and forgiving; thus, in turn, being able to give and receive love from others.

Throat Chakra

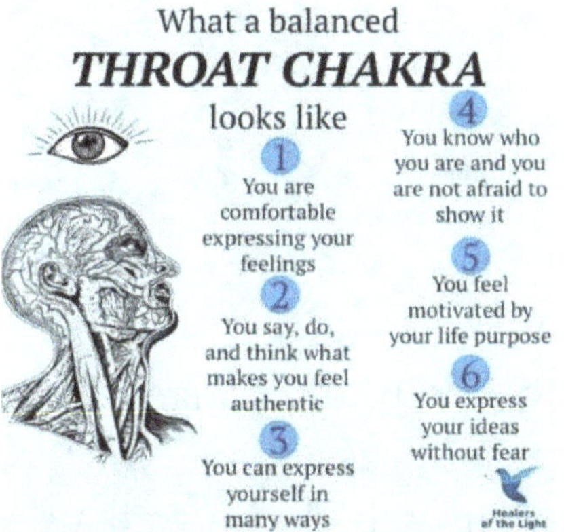

The fifth chakra on our list is the throat chakra, being the color blue. This chakra teaches you to speak your truth and be discerning over your expressions. Working with this chakra will help control your breathing and communication, making you more confident and expressive. A good way to reach this is through practicing the *Easy* yoga pose (with chanting), and some supported shoulder stands. Opening this chakra improves your communication skills, and as a result, you become more communicative and learn how to express your feelings better.

Third Eye Chakra

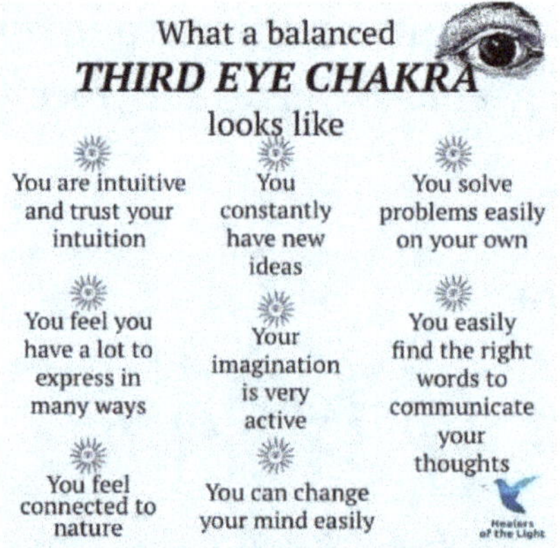

The next chakra gate we need to open is the third eye chakra which is indigo. This is the second to last chakra gate that helps us change our worldview. You open this gate by assessing your priorities and comparing them with the overall world. The yoga exercises for this chakra gate are the *Dolphin* pose and *Lotus* pose. Apart from this, you also need to increase your spirituality and intellect. This can help you open the third eye. When the third eye opens, you become detached from this world and all the other useless worldly things surrounding you. You become imaginative and connected to nature and develop a broader perspective on life.

Crown Chakra

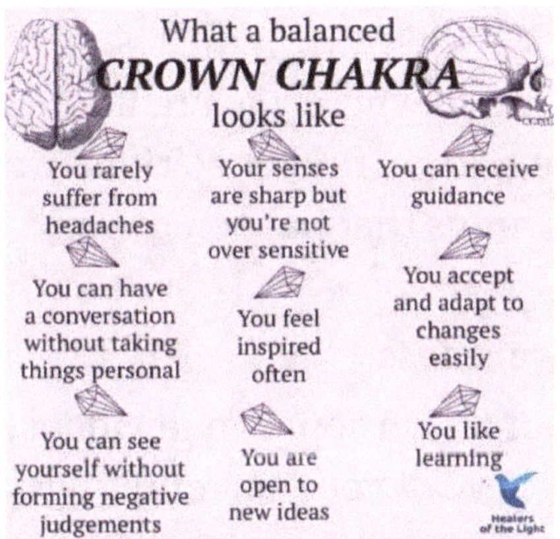

The last chakra is the crown chakra which is connected to the mind and is the color white/violet. This is the center point of all spirituality and where our spiritual 'self' lives. It is also known as the thousand-petal lotus chakra. To open this gate, you need to connect to the outside world and learn to control all of your emotions.

A good way to do this is by practicing the *Corpse* and *Lotus* yoga poses. You can become enlightened and have many energetic thoughts through this chakra opening. You become open to new ideas and ways of life. You do not take everything personally and learn to forgive others. You develop a fondness for learning new things.

The Spiritual Dimensions

There are three main spiritual dimensions of awareness.

Contracted Awareness

This is the state where you are limited to what you see. You struggle to find the 'right way' and start questioning things that happen to you.

Expanded Awareness

Your field of vision somewhat widens, giving you a better perspective of your surroundings. You begin to solve the numerous issues you previously faced and get the capacity to pay closer attention to the people in your surroundings. The qualities of love, empathy, and forgiveness grow at this time.

Pure Awareness

You undergo a profound personal transformation in the level of pure consciousness. You can quickly solve all the problems as you find yourself liberated from all the difficulties and hardships of life. You start connecting with more than just the people and the environment around you. Your entire worldview and perspective on life are altered. You experience all the pleasures of life and feel whole as a person.

Spirituality Today

The goal of spirituality is not to isolate oneself from the outside world. While many people undergo introspection that necessitates some kind of seclusion, the largest obstacle is applying your spiritual beliefs to contemporary life.

You should develop the ability to react appropriately to any situation or person that comes your way. When you respond with compassion, love, kindness, and delight, a new world will start to appear in front of you.

174

CHAPTER . 15

Indicators

"I asked for strength and God gave me difficulties to make me strong. I asked for wisdom and God gave me problems to learn to solve. I asked for courage and God gave me dangers to overcome. I asked for love and God gave me people to help. I received nothing I wanted. I received everything I needed."

—Inayat K.

Spirituality, as we covered in the last chapter, is the idea of having faith in something greater than one's self. It attempts to provide answers to queries regarding the purpose of life, interpersonal relationships, cosmic riddles, and other aspects of human existence.

A worldview based on spirituality holds that there is more to life than what humans can experience on a physical or sensory plane.

It implies that there is something more substantial linking every living creature to each other and the universe as a whole.

It could incorporate religious customs that revolve around the concept of a superior being. A comprehensive view of one's relationship with others and the wider world may also be included.

Many people have found solace and stress reduction through their spirituality. Research has revealed that while there are many ways for people to find God or a higher power, those who are more religious or spiritual and use their spirituality to deal with difficulties in life reap many benefits for their health and well-being.

Spiritual Indicators

As I just indicated, spirituality is not just one route or set of beliefs. There are several methods to engage in spirituality and gain its advantages. Your definition of spirituality will differ from others' definitions of the term.

Some define spirituality as accepting a higher power or a particular form of organized religion. Others may relate it to feeling a connection to a higher power or a sense of interconnectedness with other people and the natural world. Common manifestations of spirituality include:

Asking Deep Questions

You start to doubt several aspects of your life at this time. You start to consider nature and its nearly flawless laws.

Who produced them?

Does this have a creator?

What occurs when we pass away?

All of these queries assist and develop a connection to nature and this world, leading to a greater comprehension of things.

Deepening Connections With Other People

You start to become interested in your community. This can be helping out at your neighborhood food bank, or clearing your neighbor's pathway, etc. You attempt to see things from the viewpoint of someone you previously regarded as different. For example, instead of passing judgment on someone, you may start by asking them why they have chosen certain tattoos, concealed their faces, or some other form of self-expression you may feel is 'different' from your own.

You grow in empathy and a sense of oneness with others as a result of your willingness to lend a hand without asking for anything in return. You are interconnected with the earth. Realizing that littering, using plastics, or throwing away food is no longer a respectable personal behavior may surprise you.

Experiencing Compassion and Empathy For Others

Your capacity for empathy allows you to experience other people's emotions and adopt fresh viewpoints. Your empathy serves as the motivation for your act of compassion. Spiritually waking individuals start to perceive more all-encompassing empathy and more action-focused compassion that seems normal, natural, and rewarding.

Experiencing Synchronicity

A growing relationship with one's spiritual self is frequently linked with the perception that everything in the universe is working together to bring about a certain outcome. Consider the following scenario: Your buddy indicates that they were recently in New York over the weekend, your new neighbor has a New York license plate, and when you turn on the TV, a travel advertisement for the city is playing.

Some could dismiss this as coincidence, while others think that these imperceptible cues are pointing you in the direction of something bigger. They may interpret it as the universe letting them know that there is something in New York waiting for them.

Feelings of Awe and Wonder

You are in awe at the extraordinary manner in which the universe is created, and events take place. You wonder why objects with the same physical rules may have different natures. You wonder at the ties families provide for us, enabling us to go above and beyond for one another. These are indications that your relationship with the universe and the world around you is deepening.

Seeking Happiness Beyond Material Possessions

You have attachments, whether you realize it or not. By your attachments, you define who you are. The type of car you drive, the type of shoes you wear, what you eat, who you spend time with, who you vote for, what you read, and how you spend your money may all be ways that you identify yourself.

Since you may have gotten accustomed to them, some of these attachments or tangible belongings may hold significance in your life. But if you adopt a more spiritual perspective, you see that they are not required. Although they are a part of your way of life, they are not a need, and you can live without them if necessary.

Seeking Meaning and Purpose

You have now located or recognized the majority of the dots. All you need is a mentor or a means of making sense of things by connecting all these disparate dots. To make sense of what you are going through, you could find yourself using the internet, reading voraciously, and consulting monks, priests, or other clerics.

Wanting to Make the World a Better Place

"Look again at that dot. That's here. That's home. That's us..." said Carl Sagan when viewing the 'Pale Blue Dot' – a picture of the Earth from Saturn.

This statement captures the essence of what it means to be awakened. You realize that humanity doesn't play a large role in the grand scheme of things. Everything in your life that has happened barely occupies a pixel in that blurry image. You understand that this world is our only home, and we need to stop destroying it and change it for the better.

Once more, not every person expresses or experiences spirituality in the same way. Each of us has had a distinctive upbringing with our own distinct experiences. Even two brothers raised in the same home will have divergent worldviews because of distinct life experiences. The fact that there are so many paths to spirituality explains this. While some individuals may be more open-minded and only look for spiritual experiences in certain situations or particular places, others may be more *chill* about the subject.

For instance, some individuals may be more prone to have spiritual encounters at churches, mosques, or other religious institutions, while others may experience the same emotions when out enjoying nature on a stroll.

Spiritual Health

The path to spiritual wellness is via spirituality. A person's spiritual health will unintentionally improve when they focus on activities that speak to their spirit. Anything related to a person's spirit's health and well-being is referred to as spiritual health.

While the notion of spirit is derived from something within a human that cannot be seen in the body and is not a part of the mind, it may be described in various ways across different religions and civilizations. Many think that linking one's spirit to a deity, the energy of the cosmos, or another planet/dimension/realm, to mention a few, is the key to balancing one's physical, mental, and social elements. A person's religious or spiritual knowledge of themselves and/or the universe is often connected to the idea of spiritual health, which is wide and incorporates bigger belief systems. However, this term is related to spiritual wellness in that the individual's spiritual connections and beliefs support their ongoing physical and emotional well-being.

Our spiritual health improves as we mature on our spiritual path. Numerous signals along the path assist us in assessing our progress. The following are some indicators to watch while building a spiritual purpose:

Stable Mind

How much control do you have over your emotions? If you can manage them, that is a sign of progress, as it will indicate the opening of your chakra gates. On the other hand, if you cannot manage your emotions, that can indicate that something is wrong.

Reflecting on the Meaning of Life

Finding answers to questions like your purpose and why you are doing certain things can be a positive indicator. In addition, you may see yourself coming across new questions as you answer old ones, expanding your view of the world.

Forgiveness

As you mature along in your spiritual journey, you come to terms with the things that have happened in the past and learn to forgive yourself and others easily.

Empathy

You feel connected to your surroundings and the people around you. You can relate to them on a personal level.

Having these signs indicate that you are progressing in your spiritual journey. On the other hand, if some of these areas are regressing or are not making progress, you may have missed out on something in your spiritual journey. Remember, when you embark on your spiritual journey, the first thing you define is your spiritual journey's purpose. This definition of purpose that you assign is unique to you and acts as your road map.

Know that as long as you consciously take the necessary personal steps toward spiritual growth, you will indeed see progress. You will realize that progress when you complete the first checkpoint and feel a sense of satisfaction and fulfillment.

Spiritual Health and Spirituality

As in the comparison of eating and exercising to preserve physical health, the notion of spirituality plays a significant role in a person's spiritual health. For instance, a person who practices Christianity could attend church each Sunday, pray first thing in the morning and the last thing at night, bless their meals, and recite the rosary.

They retain that element of their health because these rituals let them connect with the higher power they believe in. The same may be said about those who adhere to pagan traditions by observing The Wheel of the Year, using the moon's phases to bring about their aspirations, and engaging in daily or weekly rituals, including using tarot/oracle cards or spell casting. This type of faith and prayer lays the groundwork for a person to develop a strong spirituality and a sense of belonging to their world, their deity, and/or the universe in general. A person might be spiritually sound without adhering to a particular faith or practice. Generally speaking, the concept emphasizes spirit, but it also has a connection to a person's life goal. Many people discover their own paths that give rise to intrinsic beliefs that enable reflection and comprehension.

Many people believe they have a purpose in life that is unrelated to a deity, a religion, or a set of rituals, and that's all ok, especially ones that involve helping others. In order to have a healthy existence, a person must experience a stronger connection to ideas like comfort, hope, and serenity. This is the goal of spiritual health.

Inner Self

Our inner self or our spiritual self is what really controls our lives. Sure, the outer self, the body, does the main work, but the inner self is where your soul lives. The soul is the real you that remains invisible. Freeing your soul is an important part of our lives.

When we connect with our inner selves, we become whole. This helps us make better and more sound decisions, improving our connection with others around us, including family, friends, office colleagues, and partners. We also become more open to changes and listen to what others say. One important thing to note is that all these changed aspects are connected. People cannot be opposed to change and still improve their lives (there is no growth in comfort). Similarly, you won't achieve much socially if you are not open or helpful to others.

If you stabilize your inner self, you don't need outside validation. When you start helping others and take a genuine interest in them, you realize that they are not that different from you, and you begin helping others out of love and not out of obligation or for the need to be validated. Having a stable mind is another part of this entire puzzle. You appear empathetic when you can process your thoughts and make time for others. Empathy shows that you genuinely care for others, especially your partner. When you can listen to others and give them good advice, they learn to trust you and realize what you tell them is for their benefit. Building trust between you and your partner is the groundwork for a healthy relationship. Also, when you become mentally stable and sound, you become open to other people's ideas because your ego isn't blocking you, allowing you to become open to change. This is because when you are open-minded, you become receptive to new ideas that show a better way of doing things, paving the way for your growth and mental maturity.

CHAPTER.16

Dependence of Personal Relationships on Spirituality

Cultivating the perfect relationship with the right person isn't always easy. However, relationships rooted in a spiritual connection may have a greater chance of success, positively impacting the satisfaction levels one feels. When the couple is bonded through their spiritual beliefs and practices, there is a mutual focus on supporting one another.

Alternatively, people who do not focus on the spiritual side do not always have fulfilling relationships. Ignoring the spiritual side can block certain, if not all, of your chakra gates, adversely affecting your relationship.

Relationships

In the most basic sense, a relationship relates to an interaction between two or more individuals. It could be anything, from a connection or association with someone to emotional or sexual interaction; all of these are different types of relationships. These could be blood-related or through other means like marriage, professional, casual, etc. Each of them has its characteristics and plays out differently.

Association

An associational relationship is a sort of formal relationship. It is the most basic form of a relationship as it only establishes a link between two people. It is what we call a weak relationship. People you may run into frequently but who are neither friends nor family are considered acquaintances. Greeting your neighbors in passing, your coworker at work, or someone you have met a few times at a social gathering but do not know well yet, are all examples of associations.

This type of relationship is symmetrical, making it one-way. These generally tend to be based on something that benefits both parties. This means that symmetrical relationships can be made or broken at will.

A good example is your relationship with your dentist or local shopkeeper. Both the dentist and the shopkeeper entertain multiple customers a day. Similarly, you can visit any other store or consult any other dentist. The relationship's only binding factor is the products and services they offer. Additionally, these products aren't limited to them; you can end your relationship and go to a different dentist anytime. All of this makes an associational relationship rather linear. There are no complications in ending the relationship and no attached emotions. Since it has none of these things, it lacks depth, making it the most basic form of a relationship. There is little to no physical contact and very little interaction, limited only to an occasional handshake, a smile, or a hello.

Friends and family

A family consists of your parents and siblings, whom you may have seen daily, as well as distant relatives like your cousins, aunts, uncles, and grandparents. Maintaining open lines of communication with family members is critical since, if a positive relationship is fostered, a family may serve as the primary source of support that can last for a lifetime.

A person's capacity to create friendships, romantic connections and other interactions outside of the family unit may also be greatly influenced based on their connection to their family. Family members often show physical affection through actions like hugging, kissing on the face or forehead, patting the head or tousling the hair, patting on the back, etc.

Friends are people we choose to engage with even when we are not related to them. Friends are people we value, admire, respect, feel comfortable confiding in, desire to spend time with, and trust. Honesty, support, and loyalty should be the foundation of every lasting friendship. A friendship is a two-way street; for it to exist, both parties involved must view the other as a friend. There are also different levels of friendship. Certain friends feel closer to you than others. This is quite typical. Some friends might not be the best people to confide in regarding private matters or worries, particularly if you have just recently met them or don't see them regularly. With individuals you've known longer or spent more time with, you can discover that you may feel more secure and can better confide in them. Good friendships include shared interests and viewpoints and are mutually courteous and helpful.

While some friendships can be intimate, and you may feel comfortable enough to greet one another with hugs or cheek kisses, other friendships may not include physical contact or only involve shaking hands. It is often inappropriate to have romantic or sexual interactions with others throughout a friendship.

Romantic

Mutual trust and acceptance of sexual needs usually form sexual or intimate relationships. These types of relationships are a combination of emotional, care, and trust-based characteristics.

In a romantic relationship, you experience a strong attraction to the other person—often both physically and emotionally. This is reciprocated by the other party in the connection. A boyfriend and girlfriend, a boyfriend and a boyfriend, a girlfriend and a girlfriend, and spouses or life partners are all examples of romantic relationships.

In a love relationship, people see each other often and may frequently communicate while they are away, such as over the phone. Many couples that live together have romantic ties. Successful romantic relationships are based on common interests, love, trust, respect, support, and a desire for the partners to spend the rest of their lives together. Having children is a decision that some individuals in partnerships make.

The duration of a relationship can vary from person to person. Some relationships may end after only a few months because it immediately becomes clear that the two people are incompatible and do not want to continue. In other situations, the couple may spend their whole lives together or be together for a long time.

In all relationships, fights and disputes are bound to happen occasionally. In solid partnerships, these disagreements can be resolved via clear communication, comprehension, and compromise, but in other situations, particularly if there are persistent disagreements, the two parties may opt to end the relationship.

Spirituality and Relationships

As we discussed earlier, relationships are interactions of two souls on the most basic level. When we seek any type of relationship with someone, it is mostly because we feel comfortable with them. We think and feel that they are suitable for our physical and emotional health. These are the things we consider when entering a relationship. However, spirituality plays an essential role in maintaining this relationship, especially spiritual health.

Spiritual Health and Relationships

Spiritual health is an important part of your relationship. It helps both you and your partner focus on yourselves. And one of the most crucial elements of a partnership is commitment. People might experience a great deal of uneasiness as a result of uncommitted relationships. People could follow current trends, but most people lack the mental stability to deal with unpredictability.

Being in a spiritual relationship makes you aware of your partner's physical and spiritual needs, as well as their emotional needs. This happens after you spend time together, meditating, opening your chakra gates, and doing other things; you start to feel a sense of the other person. This then leads you to feel more spiritually comfortable around the person. You know that whatever you say to them, they will sincerely listen to you as they know what you have been through and love you for the person you are.

When love is a natural part of who you are, it permeates all facets of life, including interactions with other people. A long-lasting, fulfilling relationship requires a sense of oneness, which faith and spirituality foster.

Only when one views the other as an extension of oneself—essentially when there isn't an "other"—can you develop a good connection. Therefore, spirituality is crucial in respecting the other person and committing to one another.

Now it doesn't mean they will always have the answers to everything and tell you the best solutions because their lives are in order. No, sometimes, you cannot put your chaotic life in order. Instead, you simply find your spirituality through emotional balance and self-reflection and accept yourself as you are.

To others around you, it may seem like you have everything in your life sorted out. But that may not be true. You may not have the answers to everything but know that everything will sort itself out in its own time, given that you follow your intuition on how to work through it.

Relationships; Past, Present, and Future

When we meditate, we clear our thoughts. We put the different volumes of thoughts in our minds on shelves in an orderly manner. We're able to travel through time as our thoughts take us to the past, helping us remember what happened. Once you meditate enough, you realize that what's in the past has passed, no matter how bad or how much it hurts you. The lessons you learned from that experience, trauma, and struggle made you and shaped you into the person you have become. Changing the past would mean that you change who you are and wouldn't be able to learn from those mistakes and challenges.

"History repeats itself" is a quote that I'm pretty sure you have heard countless times. If you do not learn from your past mistakes, history will repeat itself. This doesn't mean what happened will happen exactly as before. No, but similar challenges will surely arise.

Take, for example, relationships; if you date someone who is not the most stable person, after some time, you may leave them and date another person with similar qualities. Since you didn't learn anything from your past and that particular personality, you ended up making similar mistakes by dating similar people. If you learn from your past mistakes and understand why your relationship has ended, then you are less likely to repeat the choice you've made in partners. This is where spirituality helps; as you process your thoughts, you can realize what part you played in the relationship and what you could've done differently. Subsequently, you'll implement what you've learned into your current relationships and have better experiences.

Problems are a part of your life; even if you become spiritually enlightened, your problems won't disappear. However, you can better face these problems once you recognize the 'red flags' in a relationship that you know you should stay clear from. Your spiritual journey helps you deal with these ongoing and frequently incoming problems. It will help you find the answers because you will learn discernment, balance, and trusting intuition.

Going within, focusing on mental peace and balance, and making it a daily practice will help solve your problems and will affect your relationships in positive ways, as this relieves stress on both, the relationship and your partner.

When you are stressed, anyone who really cares for you also feels stressed and worn out. Your problems become theirs. This could negatively affect the relationship because it adds stress for your partner, who may be forced to give up and leave or stay and suffer. If you have most of your troubles sorted out, you can slowly help guide your partner, if possible, to solutions. But, you can be more accepting of the mistakes or shortcomings of your partner if they can sort these issues themselves.

There is no one alive on Earth who is perfect in every way; everyone has their own problems and scars to deal with.

You have to help your partner in the present and stick by them in their time of need so that they're there to help you if you ever need them. But be a person who is capable of handling their own issues, and not expect your partner to have to 'save' you. All of this helps the growth of your relationship, just like how learning from your past mistakes helps you in the future.

Spiritual Growth and Relationships

Both you and your partner will grow together if you practice spirituality together. Since you both experience everything together, you'll also mature in unison.

Although it is a personal journey, spiritual growth is essential in moving forward in your relationships in harmony. It gives you and your partner time to reflect on the relationship and continue looking at ways to improve individually and as a couple. A time will come when you realize the importance of your relationship; you can come to terms with any discontent with your partner by just communicating.

Talking and laying everything out on the table helps smooth things out and eliminates miscommunication. You will have a better understanding of who your partner is.

Spiritual growth also opens your eyes to the fact that your partner has their own life. They have friends and might like to do things you may otherwise not like, which is okay. They will like things based on their experiences in life, and our experiences are unique to each of us. It's healthy to continue our personal growth by spending time with ourselves and with our 'tribe,' growing and learning in our individualism, and having a partner that supports that because they're on their own journeys. Expecting or forcing your partner to make choices just to appease you isn't healthy for either person in the relationship. Focus on growing spiritually and giving your partner their own space. You shouldn't force them to spend all their time with you, and you have to accept that they are their own person, and so are you.

All of this happens when you strengthen your spiritual connection with yourself before committing to having a partner. Maintaining your spiritual connection comes from exploring spirituality individually and growing together in your spiritual beliefs and practices. Your relationship will deepen, and you will feel more secure and healthy within it. When you unconditionally trust your partner and talk to them rather than directly jumping to conclusions, you develop trust and faith in them. Even if there seems to be an issue or concern, you trust that it was either a mistake or miscommunication or they had strong reasoning behind it. All of this contributes to creating a healthy and lasting relationship. Once you develop a strong connection, you can look at a person without the rose-colored glasses on. Sure, they might have flaws, but you can see them, and you can deal with them because you know they're only human, just like you.

CHAPTER . 17

A Healthy Spiritual Life and Its Outcome

THE DEGREES OF WELLNESS

"Health is a state of complete harmony of the body, mind, and spirit."

−B. K. S. Iyengar

Spiritual enlightenment gives meaning to our lives as it makes us more aware of our surroundings. Surrender is the ultimate goal of every spiritual practice. You might equate the word "surrender" with failure or weakness, but when applied to spiritual enlightenment, it is the most potent spiritual activity since it gives you limitless freedom and opportunities. When it comes to spirituality, surrendering equates to having faith that God, a higher power, or the universe can help you achieve anything, even when you cannot predict how a situation will turn out. At the spiritual level, nothing ever happens how you want it to; everything will always unfold flawlessly in its own time. Your ego mind is the only thing that thinks you are a lone survivor in a dangerous environment when in reality, you are a spiritual entity with a spiritual 'team' to support you in this lifetime. You have to eliminate your doubts and fears, as well as the barriers your ego has built, build a trusting relationship with yourself and cultivate the guiding light within.

Spiritual Life

Our spiritual connection is strengthened and our lives are more balanced as a result of living a life rooted in gratitude and service. We become more adept at handling numerous problems as our connection and awareness of our higher selves deepen. Although we may be surrounded by turmoil, we are able to keep our composure and stay unmoved at our core. This is similar to the calm in the middle of a hurricane. We strengthen this connection to our spiritual selves by learning how our own internal signals work.

Our bodies can tell us many things when we pay attention. As energies around us shift and change, our bodies sense these changes and send us signals. These signals could be chills on a certain body part, a smell or fragrance coming about, or maybe a twitch in your eye. If these or other subtle things happen on a somewhat frequent basis, or if you can find a pattern of events when this happens, then you are learning to trust your body to tap into a universal consciousness to tell us what we need to know. This is something each of us can learn to do.

People without a connection to the 'spirit' or their higher selves may frequently feel lost or may quickly become agitated by unforeseen events in their environment. When aligned with our best selves, we have a clearer sense of who we are and a stronger sense of direction that helps us navigate life. We can carry on our life's path instead of choosing to remain victims whenever tragedy strikes or our hearts are torn apart. In such instances, we can dig deep and find our strength and positivity. We embrace the prospects of our futures, as uncertain as they may be, as we take in the splendor and beauty of life.

This sensation makes you feel complete. The gaping hole in your soul is no longer there, which was making you opt for instant gratification instead of true fulfillment. You gain inner strength, greater psychological well-being, better health, reduced hypertension, reduced depression, and the ability to handle stress. All of this is a result of a person finding their spiritual self. These aspects have already been discussed in the previous chapters, but to give a general overview:

1. The opening of your chakra gates helps in the flow of cosmic energy, which results in improved health.

2. Meditation helps clear the mind, bringing calm and tranquility to the soul.

3. Focused introspection allows you to ground yourself and helps you hone in on the many relations in your life and get in touch with them.

These practices go a long way when it comes to improving one's health. This isn't only limited to spiritual health, as spiritual wellness also affects the physical body. When a person leads a spiritual life, they are less prone to suffer from anxiety, depression, headaches, etc.

Physical ailments are thought to originate from the negative, stagnant energies in our auric field that, over time, gets absorbed and manifested within the body.

Spiritual Health

Spiritual health is an important part of spirituality as it creates a balance between the physical, psychological, and social aspects of human life. It directly corresponds to your spiritual journey. Understanding and accepting your relationship with yourself and others are essential components of spiritual wellness.

It also brings the knowledge that your life is meant for something greater than material possessions and fleeting enjoyment. Life occurs to you, not for you, and the energy we put out is the energy we receive; therefore, spiritual well-being is the desire to do good, live gratefully, and make the world a better place. As time passes, you become more aware of your inner self and connect more deeply, thereby deepening your spiritual awareness.

When you move beyond your ego, you recognize that everyone in your life is their own person, unique in their own way. No two people are alike, as all of us are subjected to different experiences in life, which play a major role in shaping our worldview and personality. Sure, many people have a lot of similarities, but that doesn't mean they are the same.

This outlook helps us better understand our partners, family members, friends, and acquaintances. You become more patient with them and help them through their difficulties, which may result in fewer conflicts and improved relationships. Accepting their uniqueness means you value them for who they are.

Responsibility

Responsibility weighs differently on every person. Some are more aware of their actions, ensuring that they don't cause harm to anyone. If they do end up harming others or making a mistake, they are quick to rectify it. Many people who go through a spiritual journey tend to become more responsible.

This results from having a deeper understanding of their surroundings and realizing that their actions have consequences. This self-awareness makes them see the world through a different lens. They consciously respond to stimulants in their environment with the intent of betterment for all of those they come in contact with. Such people view everything from a new perspective, be it relationships, responsibilities, or work. Part of this growth requires them to own up to their mistakes and face the consequences of their actions.

Coping Mechanism

There are a lot of coping mechanisms that people develop to deal with the trauma in their life. For example, they may use alcohol, smoke, make jokes about it, etc., to help with the grief of their loss.

However, no matter how many coping mechanisms they use to escape a situation, the situation won't disappear. If someone has died, or is severely unwell, then making jokes about the situation wouldn't miraculously cure them or bring them back to life, and may be considered insensitive.

Instead, facing the problems head-on and looking for consequent solutions is better than burying one's head in the sand. Sometimes, a person cannot face everything on their own and may require outside help. Visiting a psychiatrist or psychologist is one way of getting outside help. Many spiritually grounded people also try things like meditation or turn to a higher power like God or the source to whom they pray for relief. The idea is to live in the current moment, not bound to the past. The goal is the present moment of peace, love, and gratitude and sitting in the essence of that energy with a clear mind devoid of racing thoughts. Once you attain that meditative state, your mind, body, and soul undergo transformations and upgrades.

This doesn't mean that all your life challenges will be over. On the contrary, as long as you live, you will have new challenges to overcome, learn, and grow from. However, this journey helps make you stronger, makes you more mature, and able to face different challenges in life. It is important to remember not to get stuck in the past by shying away from all the responsibilities and challenges that might come your way.

Instead, stand up to them and face them head-on, not with fear but courage. These challenges are what make growth possible. Spirituality enables you to face these challenges with balanced emotions.

Spiritual Wellness

A collection of ideas, values, principles, and morals that give your life meaning and purpose is what spiritual well-being means. Your decisions in life will be determined by this and your sense of belonging to something bigger than yourself. A person may enhance their overall well-being by concentrating on a few important areas, one of which is spiritual wellness. Finding strategies and methods that work for you is ideal since they may improve your life in various ways.

Our level of spiritual well-being, or lack thereof, can significantly impact our daily well-being and capacity to handle life's stresses. According to studies, those who identify as spiritually inclined had reduced levels of anxiety and depressive symptoms, as well as physical indicators of better health, such as lowered blood pressure.

Greater Spiritual Growth

When we engage in spiritual activities like meditation, prayer, or just taking a break, we widen our minds to new ideas and viewpoints on life. As a result, we could develop a new perspective on the world and a deeper spiritual knowledge.

Inner Peace

One major advantage of spiritual well-being is mental tranquility. We can experience a sense of serenity and relaxation that help us better manage stress and anxiety when we make that connection with our spiritual side.

Better Lives and Relationships

A life that has been spiritually enhanced is frequently more content and meaningful than one that has not. When we connect with our spiritual side, our hobbies and passions may be more closely aligned with our spiritual values, such as honesty, trust, compassion, and generosity.

In contrast to individuals who are not spiritual, spiritual people also tend to have happier and more satisfying relationships. This is probably because they value relationships more and tend to be more sympathetic and understanding.

Connection With Your Surroundings

People who seek spiritual well-being frequently interact with people who hold similar beliefs. This may foster a feeling of community and support, making it easier for you to meet individuals who share your interests and feel more socially connected overall. This might entail going to a yoga class once or twice a week or occasionally attending retreats and seeking mentorship and coaching.

Improved Health

Spiritually grounded people frequently make connections with other people who hold similar beliefs. This may foster a sense of belonging, and the support you receive will enable you to meet individuals who share your interests and overall feel more socially connected.

These lessons ultimately add to the character you are building for yourself. Your spiritual team is there

– beyond your orbital vision, to assist you – waiting for you to acknowledge them and ask for their help.

Accept them into your lives, and listen to their answers through meditation.

Personal Assessment: IV

Directions: Circle the number that applies to you for each statement. Then, total up the number for each of the four columns. Write the sum of all your totals in the light gray box to the right of the chart. This number is your score for that dimension (out of 40).

Domains of Spirituality	Rarely, if ever	Sometimes	Most of the time	Always
I take time to think about what is important in life – who I am, what I value, where I fit in, where I'm going.	1	2	3	4
I feel good about myself and believe others like me for who I am.	1	2	3	4
I have a belief system in place (religious, agnostic, atheist, spiritual, etc.).	1	2	3	4
My values guide my decisions and actions.	1	2	3	4
I have a sense of purpose in my life.	1	2	3	4

	Rarely, if ever	Sometimes	Most of the time	Always
I am tolerant and accepting of the view of others.	1	2	3	4
I often meditate or listen to music, exercise to relieve stress	1	2	3	4
I often feel drawn to nature or things related to it.	1	2	3	4
I feel comfortable in the space I occupy.	1	2	3	4
You are happy with the way your life is going.	1	2	3	4
TOTAL				

Indicators	Rarely, if ever	Sometimes	Most of the time	Always
I know my purpose in life	1	2	3	4
I am able to understand the people around me	1	2	3	4
You are able to understand and relate to the people around you	1	2	3	4
I am a good judge of things and events happening around me.	1	2	3	4

I am able to control my feelings (anger, sadness, happiness, etc.)	1	2	3	4
I am able to forgive others around me.	1	2	3	4
I often find myself helping others around me.	1	2	3	4
I listen and am able to change my viewpoint without much resistance.	1	2	3	4
I often get deja vus.	1	2	3	4
I often find myself lost.	1	2	3	4
TOTAL				

Dependence on personal relationships	Rarely, if ever	Sometimes	Most of the time	Always
I am able to ask for assistance when I need it, either from friends and family, or professionals.	1	2	3	4
I am able to ask for assistance when I need it, either from friends and family, or professionals.	1	2	3	4

I accept responsibility for my own actions.	1	2	3	4
I am able to set priorities.	1	2	3	4
I work to create balance and peace within my interpersonal relationships, community and the world.	1	2	3	4
I am able to set, communicate and enforce boundaries	1	2	3	4
I can express all ranges of feelings (i.e., hurt, sadness, fear, anger, joy, etc.) and manage emotion-related behaviors in a healthy way.	1	2	3	4
I am satisfied with my relationship.	1	2	3	4
I do not let my emotions get the better of me. I think before I act.	1	2	3	4
I know what role I have in my relationship.	1	2	3	4
TOTAL				

A healthy Spiritual life and its outcomes	Rarely, if ever	Sometimes	Most of the time	Always
I find healthy ways to cope with stress (e.g.	1	2	3	4

exercise, meditation, social support, self-care activities, etc.)				
I can comfortably express all ranges of feelings (i.e. hurt, sadness, fear, anger, joy, etc.) and manage emotion-related behaviors in a healthy way.	1	2	3	4
I accept responsibility for my own actions.	1	2	3	4
I am able to set priorities.	1	2	3	4
I am satisfied with my partner and my relationship.	1	2	3	4
I am able to feel the universe calling to me.	1	2	3	4
I frequently connect with spiritual people.	1	2	3	4
I am usually able to relax and remain calm..	1	2	3	4

I have a healthy coping mechanism.	1	2	3	4
I have a healthy relationship with social media.	1	2	3	4
TOTAL				

Personal Wellness Checklist
Directions

Write down your scores from each dimension and compare them to the maximum score. You can divide your score by the maximum score to get a percentage value if that is helpful.

DIMENSION OF WELLNESS	MY SCORE	MAXIMUM SCORE
The Domains of Spirituality		40
Indicators		40
Dependence of Personal Relationships on Spirituality		40

A healthy Relationship and Its Spiritual Outcome		40

PART V
5th Dimension: Financial Wellness

CHAPTER. 18

Financial Dependence and Independence

"Financial planning and discipline is key to one's financial freedom."

—Kishorkumar Balpalli

Nowadays, more than ever, a person's quality of life is governed by the financial freedom they get to enjoy. Contrary to popular belief, financial freedom is led by two major things; discipline and planning.

Financial planning and discipline are ideas that most people only consider when considering opening a business. However, this aspect also applies to one's personal life. In a personal aspect, financial planning and discipline dictate one's financial freedom – in short, this is a concept that goes hand in hand.

Being disciplined with your finances is essential as it lays the foundation on which you can start building your financial future. Planning is just as important because it goes hand in hand with how you will grow toward financial freedom.

To achieve that, you need financial discipline, which governs your spending and saving habits. To do so, you must pay attention to specific financial goals and how soon you achieve them within a particular time limit.

These financial goals can be short-term such as:

- Clearing your student loans

- Paying off credit card debts

- Saving a small amount, etc.

Or they can also be mid-term and long-term goals such as:

- Saving up for a vacation

- Buying a car

- Saving for retirement

- Making a down payment for a house

In all these scenarios, your financial discipline will govern the outcome.

Moreover, your financial discipline can put you into two categories regarding your personal finances – you can be financially independent or dependent.

In life, you should always strive toward being financially independent. To better understand this aspect, it is good to know the difference between these two.

What is Financial Independence?

Financial independence is a term that can have different meanings for different people. For example, some might consider financial independence as the ability to retire early. In contrast, others might think of it as being able to pay all their bills without needing to borrow anything.

Similarly, for others, it relates to generating enough passive income from investments where they no longer need to work. Some people also assume that when they become financially independent, it generally means that they're living a life of luxury and comfort.

This is why it is important to ask what financial independence means to you. It is crucial to identify this because it helps you financially plan and apply discipline. This, in turn, makes it easier for you to realize your dreams.

Becoming financially independent does not always entail that you will stop working. You can still work, but instead of having it as your primary source of income, it can be supplemental.

You also have free time and the resources to pursue your passion projects. In short, achieving true financial independence can open the door to many new things for you.

What is Financial Dependence?

Financial dependency is when we rely on others for financial help to meet our needs. It's the case for most people when they're teenagers or kids. But, if you've ever been in a scenario where you had to move back in with your parents while looking for a new place, you were financially dependent upon your parents for that short period.

In such instances, you don't have the financial capacity to handle the obligations and rely on others to help pay the bills and debts.

Being financially dependent on others isn't a bad thing. In fact, most of us have, will, or are relying on someone for financial help at one point or another. Sometimes, we rely on others financially not because we want to but because we have no other choice.

Financial dependency could be due to poor financial reasons, lack of a suitable job, or reasons beyond your control. However, there is a difference between temporarily relying on others and being completely dependent on others.

In fact, financial dependency can give way to financial disorders where a person's self-esteem takes a huge hit. It's commonly seen in stay-at-home mothers, teenagers, and welfare recipients. Even though they might be at completely different levels of income, what most dependents have in common is that everything is being provided for them.

It ends up diminishing their sense of self-worth as well as stunting their economic and social skills. As a result, they end up being unprepared for the real world. Additionally, they also have a hard time managing money or understanding its worth as they have little to no involvement in earning it.

Furthermore, it can also deepen their dependency as they become used to others doing their work for them. As a result, they develop a mindset where they believe they don't need to put in the effort to do something, especially if others can do the work for them. Additionally, being financially dependent on others limits your financial power. You're unable to pursue your projects or do what you like with the money. Moreover, it might feel like the money is given to you on a conditional basis.

This dependency isn't healthy for either party – the dependent and the provider.

For example, many parents can use their kid's pocket money to exert control. In this case, when the kid does something wrong, they deduct the pocket money or don't give them anything for a certain amount of time. Such circumstances raise dependency levels and also breed resentment.

Now that you understand both, it's a good idea to strive toward financial independence.

Finances and Dating

Your finances make a difference in how your relationships develop too. In most relationships, when you meet someone, the next step is moving in together. As a result, some partners start to depend on their significant other to help them financially.

Sharing your finances is one thing, and becoming dependent on your partner is another. This, of course, puts strain on the relationship.

If a person puts the financial burden of the relationship on their partner, they're putting a lot of responsibility on their partner's shoulders and becoming financially dependent on them. It might ruin the dynamics of the relationship making it rather one-sided. This can mean the whole relationship is just one rainy day away from breaking apart.

As time passes, the financial dependency might become increasingly unattractive as their partner might seem like a burden. Similarly, the dependent person also faces self-esteem issues, minor depression, and more problems associated with poor finances.

Additionally, your financial health will dictate how attractive you look in the eyes of a potential partner. It's a given that if you're financially independent, it means that you're someone who looks after yourself, has a secure future, and in most cases, can weather an emergency or crisis. In short, it makes you look like someone stable and secure. This doesn't mean you cannot rely on your partner for help. It is alright if you are in a pinch and your partner helps you. However, if you do not work on improving your financial status, that would impact the relationship. Emotional support isn't the only thing that counts in a relationship. Fights happen because of some money problems in the relationship.

A stable relationship involves both parties discussing everything openly, including how much they earn and how much they can contribute to the relationship.

If you are financially independent, you get a voice in the relationship and can end it if it gets toxic or unbearable. On the other hand, if you depend on your partner, you might think of continuing that toxic relationship just because you do not have any other place to go.

You don't need to split the bill 50-50; if your partner pays this time, pay next time. If they don't let you pay, buy something like dessert or drinks. Just don't let your partner feel awkward or that they are pulling the entire weight of the relationship.

Financial Stress and Your Health

Financial stress is a very real thing. When you see your financial status deteriorate and you cannot make ends meet, it leads to a vast array of problems that can affect a person emotionally, mentally, and physically.

Financial stress has been linked with the following:

- Insomnia and poor quality of sleep

- Stress-based weight loss or weight gain

- Depression – mild or severe, accompanied by suicidal ideation

- Anxiety, that can lead to panic attacks or physical symptoms

- Unhealthy coping mechanisms that include drinking, taking drugs, overeating, or even gambling

- Irritability and arguments

- Social withdrawal as someone is unable to maintain their current lifestyle and entertain the same friends

- Physical ailments include migraines, gastrointestinal issues, high blood pressure, diabetes, and even heart diseases

Additionally, this creates a debilitating cycle as your poor health will mean getting high-cost medical treatment, worsening your financial state even more. Given the economic strain that the COVID-19 pandemic created, just know that you're not alone in feeling the burnout caused by financial strain.

Luckily, there are many ways that people can positively cope with financial stress.

Ask For Help

Ask for help and work with the appropriate authorities to improve your situation.

Use Healthy Coping Mechanisms

These healthy coping mechanisms include; creating additional sources of income, stress management, organizing your budget, and learning the debt cycle.

Try to Have Different Sources of Income

Different sources of income give you a boost and help you cover the extra costs you may incur.

Opt For Stress Management

Stress management helps you with your growing stress and puts you in a better mood. It also helps minimize the physical effects of stress.

Try Exercising

There are a few exercises that you can practice to relieve your added stress, including listening to calm music. However, I believe the best stress manager is organizing your budget, which helps you figure out what you need and do not need in your life.

Cut Down on Unwanted Expenses

Anything extra you are paying can be thrown out, reducing your overall financial burden.

It should be noted that at some point or other, everyone experiences financial struggles. However, how you get yourself out of that situation is entirely dependent on you. No one is obligated to fix the issue for you.

Think of it like this – if you have fallen into a pit, no one will jump down to pull you out. The best they can do is throw you a line. The rest depends on you. You'll have to work your way out. However, it should be noted that you'll actually be stepping away from dependency and moving closer to becoming financially independent in the process of doing so.

CHAPTER . 19

Effects of Financial Dependence on Relationship

We live in a consumer-driven world where everything has value, and money serves as the vehicle of trade. The home we reside in, the schools our kids attend, the vacations we take, the clothing we wear, and the food we eat all reflect our position in society, which is determined by our ability to pay.

Our social status, classes, and tiers are so ingrained in our society that they're even portrayed in popular media. Movies like *Pretty Woman* showcase the love story between a wealthy guy and a working lady, whereas, in *Titanic*, the roles are reversed. It's not unusual for two people from different social backgrounds to fall in love. The financial disparity in the movies mentioned above is huge, but with each scenario, we believe one thing – the wealthier partner will look after the other one, who no longer has to work or struggle for money.

However, it raises an interesting question: Is such a dynamic realistic? Is financial dependency healthy or unhealthy in a relationship?

Money and Its Role in Relationships

Nobody likes talking about money, and nobody loves talking about abuse, either.

Unfortunately, this means that many people are unaware that financial abuse is a problem that must be addressed. This form of emotional abuse often goes overlooked because it makes the victims feel too embarrassed to speak out about it.

When there is financial abuse, there is a power imbalance in the relationship, and the abuser uses their resources and money to control their partner.

One study indicated that 99% of domestic violence survivors experienced some kind of financial abuse in their relationships. Financial abusers increase their victims' dependence on them by limiting their financial freedom. Since their victims cannot sustain themselves, they're unable to get away and frequently return to the relationship after ending it.

Look for any warning signs listed below if your partner seems to be controlling with money, but you're unsure if you're the victim of abuse.

Your spouse controls your expenditures

Financial matters are frequently handled by a partner who doesn't let you partake in them. You have no cards, no idea what the bills are, nor know the price of normal goods. They are the ones "managing the house," and they expect you to work and then hand over your whole income to them. Even if they have a job of their own, this expectation is still there.

Your partner gets heated about money

This may occur if you bring up money with your spouse. You will be made to feel like there is no money, especially to meet your wants or needs. In most cases, if your partner is the one giving you money, they may feel entitled to you treating them a certain way and may become upset if you don't show that you're grateful because they're the ones who're giving the money to you.

You feel uneasy providing financial details

This occurs when your partner starts questioning your purchases and then confronts you about your "unnecessary" usage of household funds. It could feel easier in certain situations to just keep quiet and prevent a bigger dispute. But this sets off a cycle of mistrust and distrust in a relationship, which can ultimately result in a breakup.

The aforementioned points are a few "red flags" or signals suggesting this connection is unhealthy.

One thing I neglected to mention is that these behaviors, in addition to having a bad effect on the relationship, may also worsen your mental health by causing stress, worry, paranoia, etc. If you start to exhibit toxic behaviors to manage your partner, such a relationship may also impact your ability to maintain healthy relationships in the future.

Romance Shouldn't Pay the Bills

You understand that being in a relationship calls for more than just love—having enough money to cover living expenses might also be crucial. Can a relationship survive without money, though?

'You can earn money but never love.'

—Anonymous

This saying perfectly captures why love is the most important thing in the world. Money can only buy transitory happiness; the only feeling with the capacity to be permanent is love. You may spend money, travel the world, and feel strong, but you can never purchase love.

Sure, you might use your wealth and influence to attract others, and they could even come to "love" you as a result, but that love wouldn't be real and would only last as long as your resources did.

Feeling loved and cared for by someone else is the most important emotion in a person's life. You should never leave a loved one in quest of wealth and power when you know they care about you. There is always a method to increase your income, particularly in today's society. You won't have any trouble finding labor-intensive employment that would assist you in making ends meet even if you lack any talent but nonetheless are eager to earn money. That does not apply to love, though. There is no shop, office, or company where you can earn love. Love develops over time between two people and cannot be purchased otherwise.

Love Gives You Motivation

When you fall in love, you begin to look out for your partner and take on their obligations as well. And just having this emotion propels you forward. With love, you'll constantly be inspired to put in more effort and fulfill your partner's and your own demands and wishes.

Love Lasts Forever

Money is transient. It won't last for very long. Your wealth, status, and possessions will endure and serve as your shelter and necessities, but a home cannot be warm without love. You may disagree with what I'm saying when you reflect on your previous relationships, but this is the reality. Although it may have appeared that your love for your spouse has died, it still exists; it has simply been supplanted by other feelings like wrath or another love.

Love is a Different Feeling

You may get butterflies in your stomach or feel elated when you are with the person you love. Every time you see them, these emotions are rekindled and will last you a lifetime. On the other hand, the joy that comes from purchasing items will last only briefly.

When you purchase something you adore, you quickly become tired of it and desire to upgrade to the most recent model or find a replacement. Despite the fact that your lover is always by your side, you never seem to get tired of them. Even just being there brings tranquility and peace. There is nothing that the two of you cannot do together. Although there are certain relationships when couples get bored with one another, as we mentioned in the previous chapters, this is primarily because one or both parties are not making an effort in the relationship.

Money has no impact on concerns of the heart and mind; emotions do!

Love Cannot be Bought!

Providing your partner with financial support is very acceptable. Giving your partner money shouldn't be a huge issue; they are your buddy and perhaps your lifetime companion. You share your savings, losses, and indigence; however, is this usually the norm?

Or is it really this way? There are a lot of reasons why you shouldn't give your partner money. So should a man provide financial support for his girlfriend?

Not always.

You don't have to give your partner money if you can't afford it. Have you considered how you'll get it back if you can afford it?

You shouldn't regularly assist your partner financially for the reasons listed below:

Relationships should be equal

Relationships should always be equal, although various individuals define it differently. Some people believe that "equal" indicates a complete 50/50 share in finances; however, this is sometimes impractical or even impossible for a partnership.

What happens if neither party earns the same amount of money?

Why should they feel compelled to divide the resources equally if they can devise a different plan that works better for them?

Money might become crucial when one party is expected to keep up with the other financially but cannot do so. Clarifying expectations between partners is vital to preventing someone from feeling exploited or out of their depth in a relationship.

Don't always bail them out. Know their financial standing!

It's crucial to be aware of your partner's financial situation. It simply is. I'm not advocating that you start requesting bank statements after only one date, but if you've been dating for some time and intend to stay together or cohabitate, you don't want to have, "Surprise! I'm bankrupt!" suddenly sprung on you.

While it's perfectly okay to assist your spouse through difficult times and to have them do the same for you, you don't want to wake up one day to someone who only expects you to carry them. While your spouse may not always be in a favorable financial position, you want to know that their main objective is to be able to save money and not rely on you like a slacker.

If you consistently help your spouse out, they will rely on you to save them. You will be the support system they can rely on when things get tough. Although that is a nice thing, keep in mind that if they use this cushion (you) excessively, it will wear out. Support your partner, but remember to take care of your health and money as well. Relationship problems may arise if you cannot provide for your spouse and they become dependent on you. Once more, your spouse might not feel the need to work if you take care of the finances. They will feel less accountable to themselves if they are not in the mood to work. They won't provide any kind of financial assistance to you, but instead will rely on you and pressure you to continue serving as the household's "breadwinner."

What's worse is that they could believe that depending on you is the most they can do for the relationship and that what you're doing is completely normal. It is toxic when people believe they are entitled to your money. They will spend the money while you are held responsible for the laborious tasks.

Don't indulge/ help them with their flashy lifestyle

Love and living a lavish lifestyle are acceptable. It's acceptable to have affluent tastes, just like Anna Delvey, but you'll kick yourself later for footing their bills if they can't even afford to sustain it. You need to convince your partner to rethink their lifestyle if they constantly expect you to pay the bills or take luxury vacations. Although expensive accessories are nice, if you don't give the cost of them some thought, you might fall prey to a romance "scam."

Paying the bills or treating your partner to pricey dates every now and again, such as on anniversaries, Valentine's Day, or New Year's Eve, is acceptable. However, if they often invite you to the priciest restaurants in town, and it's not in your budget, that is an issue for you and your relationship.

The Psychology of Money and Relationships

Shared beliefs and the same objectives are prevalent features in great couples, but there is no one secret to relationship success. When the topic of personal money comes up, you'll automatically start to share your objectives and principles. These objectives and beliefs are unlikely to be completely shared by partners in a relationship, but talking about them may help you get to know your spouse and find common ground on these crucial decisions. Furthermore, these values are developed long before you receive your first income.

Everybody's "money narrative" begins in childhood, according to Dr. Alex Melkumian, founder of the Financial Psychology Center in Los Angeles, California, who spoke with Select. He said that a person's family of origin and whatever financial literacy training they get throughout their lives form the basis of their knowledge of and relationship with money.

We are all taught differently and come from different socioeconomic backgrounds. How we think about and understand money may differ greatly from person to person. Rarely do both parties in a love relationship have the same or a comparable financial background.

According to recent studies, couples who pool their finances are more likely to stay together. According to a research titled, *"Pooling Finances and Marital Happiness,"* a couple's decision to pool their finances can make or break a relationship. The study concentrated on cash and liquid assets. According to this study, couples who combine their finances are less likely to divorce than those who maintain separate accounts. So, it's crucial to talk with your significant other, regardless of your background or how challenging it could be.

Talk to Each Other!

Financial responsibility is sometimes more difficult than a simple 50/50 divide. You might make less money, they could owe more money, you might have college loans, they might have to pay child support, etc. The best course of action is to make sure you sit down and establish a list of these specific earnings and outgoings, then create a plan for how you'll handle them.

Being open and honest will help you build a solid foundation for your financial success as a partnership because arguments over money can destroy relationships. Speaking to a financial advisor might help you feel less stressed and get on the same page more quickly if you need assistance communicating or addressing problems.

Distributing Incomes

Your specific relationship and what works best for you as a couple will determine how you split your costs and revenues. Here are a few approaches individuals use to approach this task:

50/50

Keeping certain accounts with your personal assets separate may be a smart option if you appreciate the notion of working as a team but still desire to retain your financial independence.

Start by deciding which bills belong to the team and which to the individual, such as personal debt, child support, student loan repayments, and so on, and which will be handled as a team, such as utilities, rent/mortgage payments, food, etc. You can each pay the same amount to a joint bank account, allowing you to split the expenditures equally each week or month while keeping your accounts and expenses separate.

This way, you each have control over your daily spending while contributing equally to the household costs.

Proportional

Couples with glaring income disparities frequently realize that "fair" doesn't always equal numbers. You could have a stronger influence if you make more money than your spouse. Calculate your respective contributions by adding your salaries as per expenses.

Finding the total shared expenditures may be easily done by adding up all your shared expenses. Then you calculate each person's share of your combined income by adding your two incomes together. For instance:

Income Person 1: $10,000

Income of Person 2: $5,000

The combined income is: $5,000 + $10,000 = $15,000

Person 1's proportion of the income is: ($10,000 ÷ $15,000) x 100 = 67%

Person 2's proportion of the income is: ($5,000 ÷ $15,000) x 100 = 33%

According to this illustration, Person 1 pays 67% of the joint costs, while Person 2 covers 33%. By employing this strategy, the financial burden will continue to be fairly divided, even if you experience a wage increase or decrease.

All in

"All in" indicates that everyone participates actively in the financial connection and that all checking and savings accounts are integrated. You should always keep an eye on each other's actions regarding day-to-day spending and take an active role in making plans for your shared financial future.

When two individuals are on the same page and honest about how they want to spend and manage their money in the present and the future, this strategy will work well. Additionally, it permits total transparency in the flow of money.

Knowing the appropriate approach doesn't imply waiting and hoping for the best. You should discuss money with your partner frequently. You may use this to decide where you should spend more money and where you should make budget cuts.

Even though your incomes are drastically different from one another, there are various strategies to merge funds effectively. Only you two as a pair can decide what will work for you, although it can take some trial and error before you find your optimum cash flow.

Partnership in Marriage

Because marriage is a partnership, both spouses should have an equal say in all marital decisions. Additionally, there should be an atmosphere of equality in the marriage, and both spouses feel that they can have an impact on one another. This is advantageous to the relationship since it develops a sense of collaboration and makes both parties feel appreciated. Unfortunately, it frequently happens that just one spouse shares power. Instead, they absorb all the authority, refuse to listen to their spouse and act as they like. Because it makes the other partner feel voiceless, helpless, and disrespectful, that kind of conduct leads to issues.

According to John Gottman's marital studies, spouses who feel powerless or unheard in their marriage have harsher coping mechanisms for conflict and have fewer sex desires. The partnership will come to an end if the romance ends. This might take the shape of a divorce, which can cost upwards of $12,000, or a straightforward split.

Try following these easy money principles to prevent this;

1. Get a Joint Account

2. Be honest about your finances

3. Communicate with one another

4. Set financial goals

5. Legacy planning

These rules are not a sure solution to the financial problems you may face in a relationship, but they will help maintain a healthy one. You can even find your own financial solutions to the "unique" problems you face. The key is communication and understanding.

If you and your partner have these, then you will be able to sort out most of your problems without being a burden to one another.

CHAPTER.20

Planning and Budgeting 101

CHRISTINE A. BENJAMIN

"Prioritizing your savings will have you both (you and your partner) feeling financially and emotionally invested in the success of your relationship."

—Anonymous

It's not necessary for money to be a controversial topic. Regardless of whether you are a "soon-to-be," "newlywed," or "in the drains for a while," having a financial plan or budget is essential for managing your money. Budgets may appear complicated and complex, but they don't have to be. A budget is essentially an estimate of how much money you and your spouse will make over a specific period of time and how you want to spend it.

It's critical that you start budgeting together. By creating a budget, you can track your spending and combined income. Your budget not only helps you to plan and monitor where the money will be spent, but it also gives you the power to jointly control the direction of your finances.

Budget

A budget is an estimate of income and spending for a given future period of time that is often created and reviewed on a regular basis. Any organization that wishes to spend money, including corporations and governments, as well as individuals and households of any economic level, can create a budget.

Making a plan for how you will spend your money is the process of budgeting. It's a strategy for spending money. Making this spending plan enables you to estimate your financial situation in advance and decide if you will have enough money to accomplish your goals.

Making a detailed list of expenses or concentrating on a few areas may both be part of budgeting. While some like to use a spreadsheet or some type of budgeting program, others prefer to write out their budget by hand. Overall, it's important to remember that there is no right approach to budgeting; what works for one individual might not be suitable for another. Therefore, thoroughly discuss with your spouse to determine what would work best for your particular circumstances and how each of you can contribute to the plan.

Although budgeting can be a difficult issue at times, when done properly, you can succeed at it and even enjoy yourself. To make sure you achieve your objectives, your plan should be regularly reviewed, adjusted, and debated, just like all other plans. There are techniques to make budgeting more productive and less intimidating, even though it's not exactly pleasant.

Steps For a Couple Budgeting:

The first and most crucial step in creating a budget with a partner is to decide on your financial objectives. Keeping your strategy reasonable will give you a better chance of achieving those objectives.

1. Decide on Your Financial Goals, Both Individually And as a Couple

Many major, exciting things come with starting a life together. Being on the same page is essential for reducing the stress that comes with making financial decisions, and it is easier to save money when you share the same goals. You'll feel emotionally and financially involved in the success of your relationship if you put saving first.

The following objectives might help your combined budget take shape:

Paying off an Existing Debt or Loan

Any marriage should prioritize paying off debts, especially credit card debt, college loans and lines of credit. Before you merge your funds, learn the extent of your partner's debt. You can collaborate if necessary to reduce debt. Keep your funds separate while waiting for debts to be paid off. Avoid creating a joint account, cosigning, or adding your spouse as an authorized user during that period. If you want to get married, you'll need at least one solid credit history to fall back on.

Wedding

Marriage can be a wonderful, life-affirming decision. Sadly, weddings are not inexpensive! Most devoted couples ultimately decide to do it. Therefore, once you decide to marry, you must start planning the costs. Setting aside money for your wedding is usually a smart idea. This is because weddings may be pricey, and you do not want to spend the next ten years paying off debt.

Buying Property

A home is a key goal for many couples, especially after marriage. It's essential to consider more factors when buying a property in the long run than just the price of getting closer to your ideal home. You must include the cost of everything, including insurance, legal fees, relocation expenses, and furnishings.

To determine this, you can use a mortgage calculator. Consider checking your credit ratings to determine whether you should prioritize improving them before applying for a mortgage.

Traveling/ Vacations

What kind of shared and individual travel budgets you wish to create will determine everything. Most financial gurus advise setting aside around five percent of your salary for vacation. It is entirely up to you whether this involves traveling to Europe or a nearby state.

The appealing thing about factoring in travel expenses is that a trip becomes something you can afford and fit into your spending plan. Additionally, if you cannot take the vacation, the money becomes a surplus that may be put to other uses. The decision to include vacation or travel is a matter of personal taste; therefore, it is acceptable if you and your spouse think it is not crucial.

Children

They are adorable but use a lot of resources. If you start saving money before your children are born, creating a budget for their upbringing will be simpler. You can begin contributing to a Registered Education Savings Plan (RESP) as soon as they are born to help pay for their future educational expenses. The government will match 20% of your payments up to $500 per year, which is fantastic, and you can even apply for additional grants on top of that.

Savings

In order to figure out how to save, you and your spouse will need to be committed to long-term goals. If something unexpected happens, having an emergency fund and retirement savings are two of the most crucial things you'll need. You might even want to discuss how you'll achieve all of your objectives with a financial adviser.

Identifying Sources of Income

Your budget's foundation is made up of your available money. You must include all of your sources of income, including earnings and salaries, bonuses, rental income, grants and subsidies from the government, gifts, tax credits, etc. This will enable you to begin adjusting your strategies for reaching all of the objectives you have already stated.

Hammer Out All of Your Personal and Joint Expenses

It's time to consider pretty much everything you spend money on, both separately and jointly. Some costs are ongoing, while others are one-time. Ensure that everything is written down on a page or in a basic spreadsheet.

Start with your own personal costs, such as commuting costs, spending money on meals, and shopping. Put the monetary amount and each cost on a separate line. You may make a tentative estimate for variable costs like dining out that can be altered later. Next, discuss the shared costs. Most couples share financial responsibilities (mortgage, school funds for a future kid), assets (house, car, savings), and costs (groceries, date nights, auto insurance, utilities, even credit card interest) (car maintenance, gifts, home renovations). Review your budget objectives and confirm that each one will be covered in the budget you're going to create.

Once more, you should include each shared expenditure and its associated cash amount on a separate line in the spreadsheet. Separate columns for individual and shared spending are useful, in my opinion. In this manner, each couple is aware of their own spending habits.

How to Split Your Expenses

The most personal and difficult phase of the entire process—even for the relationship—is this. It could be a difficult task, but it won't be unpleasant if you and your partner already agree about your goals and are truthful about where your money comes from. Discussions like these are critical to assist one another in leading the lives you both desire.

Depending on the cost, you must select how much of each expenditure you will be responsible for covering. For instance, you may pay the electricity bill while your partner pays the family's cell phone bill. It's up to you how to divide the money, but it may be useful to think about topics like how income inequality may impact the quality of life or who stands to gain the most from the expense. If you require Netflix to feel joyful, but your partner is more likely to be working in the garden, you may pay for more of the expense of streaming while they pay for the majority of the perennials.

Your investment in one another may depend on where your relationship is at. You may opt to share the budget evenly or have the one who makes more money contribute more if you both strongly desire a grand wedding or want to buy a home together. It's ultimately up to you and your team to determine what works best for you. Sadly, there isn't a universal recipe. But as long as you both genuinely believe that you are in this together and are content with the strategy, it will strengthen your bond and position you to achieve your team's objectives.

Set Savings Expectations and Spending Limits

The moment has come to talk about what spending caps each person can live with. It's crucial to have a sizable buffer and a healthy dose of reality unless you want to frequently disappoint yourself or turn to credit cards when expenditures surprise you. Nevertheless, imposing restrictions is a crucial step in reducing unnecessary spending. You can see how simple it is to overspend if you know where your money is going.

After discussing your savings and cost projections, decide what amounts to enter in your spreadsheet or budgeting tool for certain goals. Moving money from one spending category to savings for a large project will be made clear by your shared budget.

Keep things in perspective by examining your spending patterns and making a few little adjustments. Maybe you can start a *Frugal Friday* where your partner takes public transportation to work and you pack a grain bowl from home as opposed to their regular preference. This will help you both cut down on your unnecessary expenses and focus on what is important.

Fund Your Budget

Having a joint checking account that acts as a shared budget account is one of the simplest ways to budget as a couple. Your spreadsheet should include a column for each of your names. Assign each partner a share of each spending. Finalize with a grand total. You may use this to determine how much money each individual should put into the joint account each month. To get at a distribution that you both feel is fair, exclude any costs you don't want to be paid from the joint account.

Invest

Even if you have limited resources for investing, you may still use your earnings to increase your income by making tiny contributions to investment accounts. Discover whether your workplace provides

401(k) matching, which is effectively free money. If you haven't already, open a retirement account or other investment account.

The first step toward improved money is altering your personal behaviors. Some of these adjustments will be simpler than others, but if you stick with them, you'll develop excellent money management skills that you can use for the rest of your life while also putting more money in your pocket. A strong budget is the cornerstone of wise money management.

Manage Your Expenses

The willingness of both partners to collaborate on a budget or strategy is crucial. Some people have never created a budget or a plan, and they start after they are married to a partner who shares their opinion. You might need to go to therapy if your spouse doesn't stick to a budget. This will help you figure out how to talk openly about money and develop a long-term strategy. As we previously said, placing all of the responsibility on your spouse can result in resentment and arguments that will ultimately lead to a split.

You may avoid sliding into debt by managing your monthly spending, which helps you be ready for life's unforeseen events. Because of this, budgeting is crucial. It doesn't have to be tedious. You don't have to be brilliant at arithmetic, and keeping track of your income and expenses doesn't mean you can't buy the items you want. Simply put, it means you'll be more aware of where your money is going.

Financial Independence and Its Outcome

Financial stability is the state of being debt-free. You can pay your bills on time each month, have money set up for retirement, and have cash on hand in case of emergencies. Being financially secure allows you to manage things on your own and avoid being a burden on your partner.

Financial Stability

Everyone strives for financial security, but few individuals truly achieve it. The concept of "financial independence" has many meanings to different people. Some individuals define financial independence as the ability to purchase whatever they choose, whenever they please. For many, it may include letting go of concerns over how they will cover unforeseen or large spending. It can simply mean getting out of debt for some, while it might entail having enough money to retire for others. Although some of these interpretations are accurate, none are complete solutions.

You feel secure about your financial condition when you are financially solid and know you will have the money to pay for necessities without worrying. You have savings for your future objectives and enough money set aside to meet emergencies.

You are largely debt-free. Being wealthy doesn't guarantee financial security. It's not even a number, really—more of an attitude. When financially secure, you can focus on other areas of your life without worrying about money.

While achieving financial stability may seem like a pipe dream, it is possible. You will need to put in the effort, which will take some time. But the effort is worthwhile. Because it may impact your entire financial health, being financially stable is vital. Paying your expenses without worry could be simpler when you feel financially secure.

Remember that financial security is a personal experience and does not always mean the same thing to different people. This occurs as a result of the fact that everyone has different financial goals and long-term aspirations.

Make Your Finances Personal

Your personal funds are private, and it's crucial to state this upfront. That doesn't imply that you can't discuss money with anyone because it's personal. Making your finances personal entails putting your attention where it belongs: on you, not on anybody else.

One of the most crucial factors in achieving financial stability is this. We continuously compare ourselves with others in our society. We are told that we must adopt a particular way of life because successful people do that. It doesn't matter whether you make more money than your buddies do. The only things that count are how much you have and how you utilize it to achieve your objectives.

Forgetting about the "proper way" to accomplish things is a crucial aspect of this guideline. The answer is that certain financial choices are generally better than others. But a lot of factors in personal finance rely on the individual. There isn't a single strategy or schedule that works best for everyone. Don't punish yourself for making the incorrect choice if you set a savings goal and fail to meet it. Just consider what transpired. What went well, and what didn't? Utilize that knowledge to get better the following time.

Your Most Important Investment is Yourself

You should aim to invest in yourself before you even consider putting money into the stock market. Spend the time, effort, and money necessary to equip yourself with the essential abilities. College degrees count here. It also contains additional skills and expertise. Sometimes, learning things that have nothing to do with your line of work can be just as beneficial to you as learning things that do. Employers often seek out individuals who can contribute to their businesses in a variety of ways. Additionally, they seek a candidate that demonstrates the motivation and ambition to advance. Your success depends on how well you feel. Medical expenses are one factor that quickly depletes resources. Even while you can't stop all diseases from occurring, a balanced diet, regular sleep patterns, and exercise can help a lot. That entails keeping your stress levels down. Find ways to unwind and relax. Sure, consider the important people in your life, such as your spouse and family, but ultimately, put yourself first. Mental, physical, and financial well-being should always come first.

To conclude, we have covered this in great detail in earlier chapters. You can't help people well if you aren't stable yourself. A person lacking stability will be a risk to others, just as a structure with solid foundations is.

Earn Income by Doing Something You Enjoy

Most people make their money primarily via employment. Therefore, finding a job that offers a stable income is the greatest place to start if you're thinking about maintaining your financial stability. The ideal situation is to work a job you like. It will be simpler for you if you work at something you like. This can entail a job change for some folks. If you don't like the personnel or structure at your present firm, it can mean switching employers. Perhaps starting a freelance business or finding a part-time job will be your answer. Although it may not seem like the ordinary course of action, your happiness (and sanity) come before anything else.

Follow a Budget

We have discussed this in the last chapter, so you should know what this means. But in short, make a plan that is precise and includes all of your expenses. Follow that plan and keep modifying it according to changing circumstances. This will allow you to save money, help you keep track of where your money is going, and show you what your expenses look like.

Live Below Your Means

This is a piece of advice that many people have heard. The issue is that a lot of us find it difficult to implement. We live in a society where we are continually told what we "should" do or spend money on. And still, spending money on extra items we don't need is often the norm. However, living within your means is the secret to long-term financial success. You can't expect to develop savings if you routinely spend all your income or more.

Budgeting and living within your means go hand in hand. Your monthly spending capacity is indicated by your budget. After that, you may use that figure to ensure you don't exceed the budget.

Create an Emergency Fund

Work on accumulating an emergency fund before you consider investing for retirement or paying off debt. Having an emergency fund might help you prepare for unforeseen circumstances. There is always a danger that you may lose your work and have to survive without a regular income for a while. Perhaps you need to make a significant auto repair or go on a trip you didn't anticipate. An emergency fund will help you overcome a difficult moment by paying for some or all of the expenses. By providing you with a backup plan, an emergency fund will also provide you peace of mind.

People may forego an emergency reserve in lieu of retirement savings. Then, when a significant expenditure arises, they are forced to withdraw funds from their retirement account to pay for it. Always use early withdrawals from your retirement savings as a last option. Your retirement funds will be reduced, and you'll probably have to pay fines.

Pay Off Your Debts

Having debt will always make it challenging to become financially stable. Focus on paying off debt once you have established your comfortable spending limit and an emergency fund. To prevent more credit card debt, pay off any outstanding balances. Do you have education debts? Make additional payments to eliminate them as soon as possible. It's not always impossible to pay off your debts earlier just because you agreed to a 10-, 20-, or 30-year payment schedule. In the long term, paying off your debt sooner will save you money since you'll accrue less interest.

The only catch is that you must have a mortgage. You have some time to pay off your mortgage if you have one. Put all other debts ahead of your mortgage in priority. You should continue making all your normal mortgage payments but prioritize paying other debts with extra funds. If you want to, you may concentrate on paying off your mortgage early once you have paid off your other debt and have amassed enough money for retirement.

Save and Invest For Your Retirement

It's difficult to consider retiring while you're young. Why put money down for something that won't happen for decades? Unfortunately, this way of thinking contributes to most people's lack of retirement savings. You must prepare for the times when you won't receive a paycheck if you want to achieve financial security. This is particularly valid if you have any retirement plans. When you retire, do you want to travel? Would you want to volunteer or attend a local course? All of those things are wonderful, but you can't accomplish them without money. Put retirement first now, and you'll be glad you did afterward. Begin your retirement savings immediately, even if you don't have much to put down. Long-term earnings are increased by starting early due to the wonders of compound interest.

Make Sure to Have Some Fun

It's simple to forget about enjoyment when concentrating on debt repayment or money savings. After all, "fun things" frequently have a price tag. But avoid being so preoccupied with the finances that you stop living. Living life to the fullest will keep you happy and healthy. Try to budget some money for fun when determining how much you can afford to spend each month. You can involve your partner in this. Maybe you and your partner could go to a performance or have massages every few months. Try fun dates and keep an eye out for affordable and free activities as well. Take a stroll with your significant other, or have a game night with pals at your house. Celebrating your financial achievements is a fantastic additional method to have fun.

Stick With Your "Long-Term Financial" Plan

In a perfect world, you would adhere to your monthly spending plan. You would never lose your job, and your automobile would never require maintenance. Unfortunately, the world is not perfect where we live. Unexpected events happen, and occasionally you spend more money than you planned. Try not to get disheartened when things don't go according to plan. Instead, adjust the plan, even when things aren't going well. Even if you lapse for a few weeks or months, keep going. Don't stress about getting everything right. Give it your best shot and strive to improve daily.

Financial Independence

Financial independence is the state of having enough money to cover one's expenses without borrowing money from others or incurring debt.

Being financially solid leads directly to financial freedom. Many of us think that being financially independent is having enough money to be able to stop working and take care of ourselves. While this may often be true, it doesn't always have to be. For starters, if you have enough money to pay off your bills by the end of the month, aka you are financially stable, then you are, for most parts, financially independent. Sure, you are still dependent on your salary and may be in a pinch if you lose your job. But by large, if you can support yourself with the salary you earn every month, you are financially independent for the time being. That is because all the money you earn is yours, you do not have to borrow it from someone, and as long as you have the said job, that money will keep flowing in.

Some of the major benefits of having financial independence are;

Prepared for Contingencies

In times of emergency, having financial independence is crucial. You won't be "penniless" in a crisis if you are financially independent and have an emergency reserve.

Freedom to Choose

You are not bound to anyone or anything. You can choose where you put your money and when to spend it. Sure, you and your partner might decide to share certain expenses, but that is like paying your bills. Other than that, your money is yours to spend. This leads to a certain feeling of happiness as you get the feeling of having accomplished something. You are not burdened or stressed by the worry of having to pay your bills on time. You know that even if something goes wrong, you will have your emergency fund to carry your expenses while you look for another job.

Stress-Free Life

Having financial freedom leads to a stress-free life. You are mostly free to make choices and are not dependent on another person. You do not have to worry about whether your partner will support you this month or not.

As I mentioned in the previous chapter, finances are the number one thing that leads to fights. Being able to support yourself means that those fights are less frequent. You and your partner may share the overall budget, but apart from that, you will have finances that are 'independent' from one another.

This will be less stressful for both of you as you only have to take care of yourself. You will not have to worry about some x, y, or z bill your partner might put forward. Sure, sometimes you may have to bail your partner out if they are in trouble, but you will not have to depend on another person to do that for you; your savings will take care of that.

Freedom of Lifestyle

Earlier in the chapter, I mentioned that one should always "live below their means" to be financially stable. Well, once you are stable, have little to no debts, have a steady income, and have good savings/ backup, you can try adopting a different lifestyle. Invest in yourself, climb the ladder of success, and slowly improve your lifestyle.

Another way you can choose your lifestyle when you are financially independent is you are the master of your own money. You do not have to live according to what another person or your partner decides for you; you can do it on your own. Similarly, you do not have to plead or negotiate with someone if you want to buy a new car, house, or something else—you can do it on your own. However, if you and your partner have a shared budget, discussing it with them before taking this step is always a good idea. But, at the end of the day, the decision remains in your hands.

Gives You a Voice

As I said in the previous point, you do not have to negotiate with anyone if you want something; you can buy it if you want to. Discussing with your partner is helpful because it avoids unnecessary conflict. A discussion can also be beneficial for you since your partner may guide you to a better deal.

PART VI
6th Dimension: Sexual Wellness

CHAPTER . 22

Recognizing Sexual Health

"Sex is an emotion in motion."

—Mae West

Sexual desire is underlined by an impulse to gratify one's own desires. In comparison, emotional concerns are less significant in sexual desire due to the deep evolutionary roots behind sex. However, the issue is made clear by fantasy's role in sexual desire.

Like all other emotions, sexual desire is a complicated web of feelings that draw you to someone. The common elements of sexual urges include motivation (the need to be with your partner), emotion (enjoyment, pleasure, stimulation, etc.), cognition (understanding the other person), and evaluation (assessment), even if numerous factors might vary from person to person.

One of the seven "positive" human emotions, sexual desire is the most potent energy of all human desires. The others are longing, trust, love, adoration, passion, and hope.

When engaging in sexual activity, many people consider significantly superior states—states that include not only their current partner and current behaviors but also their prior partners as well as their surroundings.

The majority of us are inquisitive about our sexual lives and how they compare to those of our friends, coworkers, and neighbors, even if we don't like to admit it.

Questions like;

Am I having enough sex?

How long should I stay in bed?

How frequently should I 'mix it up' every time?

make us concerned about whether or not our sexual behavior is 'normal.' Understanding and accepting every part of our sexuality is necessary for good sexual health.

Sexual Health

The first thing that comes to mind when discussing sexual health is STDs or sexually transmitted diseases. That isn't the complete picture, however. Having no STDs is undoubtedly a sign of good health, but this does not equate to having a healthy sexual life. Along with being free from sexual dysfunction, STDs, and sexual assault/coercion, sexual health encompasses feelings of self-worth, personal beauty, and competence. The affirmation of sexuality as a positive energy enhances other facets of one's life through sexual wellness. When behavior, values, and feelings are consistent and integrated within the larger personality structure and self-definition, it is referred to as having a healthy sexual orientation. This orientation to sexuality is based on correct information, personal awareness, and self-acceptance. Intimacy with a partner, open communication about sexual wants and desires, sexual functionality, deliberate and responsible behavior, and the capacity to establish acceptable sexual boundaries are all aspects of sexual health.

In addition to self-acceptance and respect, sexual health also reflects respect for and awareness of individual uniqueness and sexual culture.

When you have a healthy sexual life, you;

Feel good about your body

Always be proud of your appearance and have a good attitude toward your body. Positive ideas and feelings about physical appearance, weight, and sexual attractiveness during sex support healthy sexual function.

Are not afraid to ask for what you want

You and your spouse can't be expected to understand what the other is thinking. You still wouldn't understand what is going on in the other person's thoughts even after spending years in each other's company. Therefore, discussing such topics is usually a good idea.

You and your partner should be receptive to hearing what the other wants or needs to respond appropriately. Try texting if you have trouble being open about your sexual urges. You could discover that texting your lover about your desires is simpler than speaking to them in person or expressing them in the heat of the moment.

Plan to have sex

Sex doesn't always happen out of the blue. Sometimes, it takes preparation to create the "perfect mood." To accommodate it, one must plan and arrange other activities. This is especially useful if one or both of you have demanding jobs or young children, both of which can interfere with and limit your ability to engage in sexual activity.

Do not keep count

Focusing on certain figures is unhealthy and does not increase productivity, regardless of how frequently you do it (daily, a few times per week, or once per month). No matter how frequently you have sex, once a week or once a month, if you or your partner are unhappy, it makes no difference. Making it on the numbers rather than the satisfaction would ultimately result in subpar performance.

Enjoy and look forward to it

Observing how it makes you feel is an excellent method to assess your sexual health. If you like it, you should naturally feel good. Your relationship should bring you closer to your spouse and should feel satisfying. You don't need a crazy or wild sex life to experience these emotions. Your partner should be someone you like being intimate with. Even if you can experience an orgasm but don't actually enjoy the sex, the relationship won't progress.

Say no if you don't feel like it

It is necessary to have the "desire" to participate in sexual activity. When you don't want to engage, don't do it just because your lover asked you to. Yes, it is acceptable to receive such requests occasionally, but continuously going against what your body desires might make it seem more like a burden than a pleasure and affect your libido.

Know when to change things up

Try mixing things up a little by bringing some spice into the bedroom to prevent making it look like a routine. Simple changes, such as changing your hairstyle or wearing new underwear might be used to inject something novel into the bedroom. Even a slight change in setting may amp things up and provide some flavor. Talk to your spouse and be open to fresh ideas if you believe they are still not in the mood.

Feel happy with your partner

Your sex life is likely in good shape if you're happy with your spouse. Having an interest in having sex, feeling good about how frequently it occurs, seldom arguing about having sex, and simply being pleased with your spouse are signs that you are satisfied. Although sustaining this connection will favor the relationship, there is a clear correlation between sexual pleasure and happiness in your partnership.

Have a racy vocabulary

You don't need to climb mountains to have a fulfilling sexual life. Small acts of kindness and care that keep you romantically and physically connected are sufficient. This can take the shape of late-afternoon texts or sexy conversations. This is a fantastic approach to increase fulfillment.

Don't freak out about the occasional slow stretch

The intensity and passion of your sex life won't always be constant and will fluctuate throughout your partnership. Being honest about what constitutes a healthy sex life and how much you and your spouse can bear is crucial in all of this. Recognize that there are no right or improper sexual behaviors. Therefore, you two should be honest with one another about your feelings and your moods. You will have a healthy sex life if you consider a few essential aspects associated with it.

Sex and Emotions

Sex can be whatever you want it to be. It might be an emotional roller coaster or the height of romantic love and connection. It can also be used as a stress reliever, a means of reproduction, or just for fun. This discrepancy could result from the society in which we live. Maybe all we've done is follow what we were told was right. This may result in conflicted emotions that worsen the relationship, causing tension, worry, exhaustion, and sadness.

Some individuals find that acting on physical attraction can result in emotional attraction, while others discover that acting on emotional attraction can result in physical attraction. Regardless of your personal perspective, sex and emotion affect the same neural pathways in the brain. Most people often feel similar emotions during sexual activity and release. Certain emotions are frequently experienced during or right after sex due to the hormone surge that occurs during sex.

It's also crucial to remember that when you're aroused, your ability to reason typically vanishes. Even though we frequently miss it when it's occurring, it's clear in hindsight. Certain brain regions that support critical thought and logical behavior, such as the prefrontal cortex, might become inactive due to sexual excitement. That explains why sexual desire overrides sound judgment and thinking, carried away in the exhilaration.

Sexual and emotional problems don't just affect you; they also influence your close relationships and might make it difficult to be intimate and close.

Due to a lack of satisfaction or a fear of failing when it comes to sexual performance, you could feel distant or physically and emotionally retreat. Your companion could be concerned that you are losing interest or don't want to see your loved ones. These factors could affect both your partner's and your own self-esteem. Understanding how the various emotions might impact your sexual health can help you and your partner have more satisfying relationships.

Sex and Self-esteem

Self-worth, or how you feel about yourself, your strengths, and your limits, is what is referred to as self-esteem. This might apply to your own convictions, demeanor, feelings, and actions. Positive self-esteem also entails confidence, so if you lack confidence in who you are and yourself, you could also lack faith in your feelings about sex and sexuality. Therefore, having healthy sexual esteem will probably result in more confidence in your capacity to have the sexual experience you want.

Sexual self-esteem is commonly understood to refer to how you feel about your body and your confidence in your ability to relate to another person. It has to do with how you feel about yourself physically and emotionally. Your sexual self-esteem influences your sexual decisions. If you have poor self-esteem, everything suffers, from libido to performance.

Ways to Enhance Self-Esteem

- Accept yourself the way you are

- Take time for yourself

- Appreciate your sexuality

- Stand up for your values and beliefs

- Practice saying "no."

- Replace negative thoughts with positive ones

- Communicating with your partner

- Do some self-care

If you feel that you need to change or that you're not good enough, simply take a step back and take a moment to evaluate yourself. Find a few positive attributes, pay attention to them, and work on your one 'bad' quality if you have any. Keep in mind that you don't have to evaluate yourself against others.

Spiritual Sex

Many people use sex for a variety of reasons. It appears to provide bodily gratification and release, but that's not all it gives. The emotional connection that sex fosters between lovers can increase closeness and trust. Some individuals even go so far as to consider sex to be both a spiritual and a physical experience. Like spirituality, there are several meanings of spiritual sex as well. Some individuals believe that spiritual sex is directly related to their religious practice. Others consider it to be a particular set of spiritual rituals, also referred to as tantric sex. Others regard it as a method of engaging in sex that results in a more profound, spiritually rewarding relationship with a partner.

Spiritual sex can be accomplished in any way. With such a wide range of connotations, you can almost surely find a method to incorporate spirituality into your sexual life that is comfortable for you.

Sexual Health in Women

When your hormones fluctuate, such as after giving birth or throughout menopause, sexual issues can arise. Sexual dysfunction can also be a symptom of serious illnesses, including cancer, diabetes, or heart and blood vessel (cardiovascular) disease.

The following factors can lead to sexual dysfunction or dissatisfaction:

Physical

A wide range of illnesses, such as cancer, urinal problems, multiple sclerosis, heart disease, and bladder issues, can cause sexual dysfunction. Your body's capacity to achieve orgasm can be decreased because of medication, including antidepressants, blood pressure meds, antihistamines, and chemotherapy.

Hormonal

Your genital tissues and sexual receptivity may change due to lower estrogen levels during menopause. A reduction in estrogen causes the blood flow to the pelvic area to diminish, which can reduce genital feeling and lengthen the time it takes to attain orgasm.

Additionally, the vaginal lining gets thinner and less elastic, especially if you don't engage in sexual activity. These elements may cause dyspareunia, popularly known as painful sex. When hormone levels drop, so does sexual desire after giving birth, and while nursing, your body's hormone levels change as well, which can cause vaginal dryness and alter your desire for sex.

Psychological and Social

Sexual dysfunction can result from or be exacerbated by untreated anxiety, depression, chronic stress, and a history of sexual abuse. Pregnancy anxieties and new mother demands could have comparable impacts. Your sexual receptivity may also be affected by ongoing arguments with your spouse over sex or other elements of your relationship. Body image difficulties, cultural and religious challenges, and other factors may also play a role.

Sexual Boundaries

The line separating what you're fine with from what you're not is known as your personal boundary. You have a barrier between yourself and something if you're uncomfortable with it occurring to you or around you. How you are touched, how your body is perceived, how you are treated, and what you find comfortable may all be considered when it comes to sex.

Your expectations for intimate physical contact are known as sexual limits. What is and isn't acceptable in your sexual life? It's usually a good idea to set clear boundaries about frequency, sexual comments, unwanted touching, expectations for other people engaged in your sex life, and which sexual practices are desired and off-limits. Setting up a boundary means letting the other person know about something you feel uncomfortable with.

Healthy sexual boundaries involve recognizing each other's sexual preferences and limits, as well as mutual agreement and consent. Asking and listening to someone is the greatest way to learn about their boundaries. Even if you admire something, respect their wishes if you feel they are uncomfortable with it.

Watch for any indications of sexual coercion. When your boundaries are being crossed, take a step back and simmer down. It's possible that the person you're with doesn't respect your boundaries or is incapable of recognizing the expressed boundaries. Sexual encounters are also dynamic. You might need to clarify your limits because there was a communication breakdown. Or, you can feel uneasy out of the blue and decide to adjust your limits as you go. Absolutely no problem! A new border can be established at any moment. You get to determine what you do with your body since it's yours!

CHAPTER. 23

Letting Go of the Past

CHRISTINE A. BENJAMIN

"Every day and every moment is a chance to let go. To open ourselves up to new experiences, and to take action to create a meaningful future."

— Anonymous

Sometimes the burden of our past hangs heavy on our shoulders, delaying our development. In such instances, we are held back, unable to live in the present, and powerless to let go of the past and from pursuing our true selves. We fear that when we would let go of the past, we will enter uncharted territory and will be vulnerable. That is where the issue first arises.

It's not always easy to create a meaningful future. It takes a lot of time and effort to determine what we desire. On the other side, staying in the past looks easier since you are accustomed to it. We have to invest a lot of time and effort in letting go of the past, which makes this process appear more challenging than it actually is. Past events also significantly influence how we view ourselves.

When we let worry, anxiety and rumination rule our thoughts and influence how we behave in the present, we hinder our own growth. Clinging to the past prevents us from appreciating the beauty of the present.

And we are unable to recover and let love and happiness fill our hearts.

Therefore it's time to start letting go of the scars from our past and the memories they hold. We won't be able to go forward with a clear idea of what we desire unless we separate ourselves from those errors. Learn what you need from the past, and leave the rest behind where it belongs. We alone possess the ability to create a future in which we are unrestricted by the past.

Let the Past Flow

The mantra *"Let it go"* is one of the most oversimplified in self-help or meditation.

Being encouraged to let something go may be quite annoying, especially if we are already struggling with a bad experience. It might sometimes be difficult to understand what this truly entails.

How can we let go of something that seems so unjust, unsettling, tragic, and significant to us?

There is no quick fix to letting go, including unreasonable fears and broken hearts. It requires intentional effort to be at peace with the past and the choices you made.

Letting go is not like throwing something in the trash. Moving through the pain and unfavorable feelings that plague you doesn't make it impossible; it only means it is easier said than done.

Your Past Will Anchor You

We really hold ourselves back and stop our progress when we cling to the past and all the negative experiences. If you let it, your past will wreck your present. It will stop you from seizing new chances and from truly and profoundly loving both yourself and other people.

We must let go of the past and embrace the possibilities of the future if we are to design a life that is peaceful and fulfilling.

Recognize what went wrong and commit to creating a future where all those errors are corrected. You don't have to let the person you were yesterday define you. You can start anew and live in a truth that aligns with your beliefs and needs. Have the capacity to offer yourself a new start.

It's up to you to choose between staying unhappy or moving on. If you allow yourself to remain in your past, it will rob you of everything. You must find a way to get over your past and forgive everyone, including yourself, if you want to be genuinely happy. We have the opportunity to change the future. Either we can take charge and give ourselves a chance to be happy, or let what was, dictate what is. Some people merely go through the motions in their lives. Although they don't engage in life, they appear to be doing so. They are daydreaming, hoping, and stuck in a past life that should have occurred but never did – a horrible waste of time. If you refuse to let go, you'll never completely understand your capacity for bravery, strength, and living life to the fullest. In this instance, you deprive yourself of the opportunity to fully and abundantly experience life.

The Past is Done

The past is no longer relevant. Although what happened cannot be changed, how you choose to respond to it can. You are not defined by your disappointment, unhappiness, or battle to obtain something that was not intended for you.

Reframe your thoughts and sentiments to a more positive one to reflect on the lessons learned and wisdom obtained rather than thinking adversely about them. Then permit yourself to accept that you are a perpetual *"work in progress."* You come to view these previous experiences as stepping stones toward your future as you develop as a person.

Don't Limit Yourself

Your inability to let go is a result of self-limiting ideas. In such instances, you restrict your ability to evolve when you think what you're going through cannot be changed and is your only option. You restrict your prospects when you have low expectations.

Narrow thinking blinds you from seeing the opportunities to try something new and be successful. You deny yourself the chance to control your creative processes.

Our memories are stored in the past, but not all are conducive to leading a happy life. Our restricted views confine us in outdated mindsets that don't advance our larger objective. We have to liberate ourselves to thrive and release these restrictive ideas.

Make Space

As you release something, you make room for something new to occur. It's comparable to having a closet full of useless items.

Even so, do you know what's inside?

It's critical to pause and assess your true emotional, psychological, physical, and spiritual needs.

Do the aspects of your life that used to make sense still make sense to you?

Do you cling to the past out of nostalgia?

Do you worry you'll forget if you let go?

When the remnants of the past are removed, a huge space is left open for other good things to enter. We must feel at ease to open ourselves up and claim what is truly ours.

This can apply to new career prospects, changes in our love relationships, or even changes in ourselves.

Your Past is Not Your Identity

Although it is a part of your past and who you are, it is not who you are. Your experiences reveal aspects of who you are. Things do happen, but each person's unique perspective colors how they occur and manifest themselves.

You leave your mark on how things happen.

Your identity is a component of both your history and your future. You can't live in the present if you're stuck in the past, so stop doing that.

Conserving Energy

Clinging to the past is a huge waste of time and effort. You cannot alter anything about your history. You're wasting time and space by staying in this long-gone location instead of using that time to improve your life.

Don't waste time by dwelling on the past; it's done. It doesn't have to define you. Save your strength and concentrate on where you can make a difference.

Heal Before Moving On

It is hard to make yourself forget about unpleasant events. There are several ways that old scars may infiltrate a relationship. They may sabotage a relationship, stop it from taking flight, or gradually tug at it until it is gasping for oxygen.

Everyone has the ability to connect in a way that is loving, allows each individual to be fully seen, and bares all their masks, with all of their flaws and vulnerabilities on full display. It's lovely, yet difficult, since this kind of connection demands candor and transparency. The fortifications must crumble, and the armor must erode.

Let Yourself Grieve

Following a breakup, allow yourself to experience the emotions. Don't push yourself to "get over it" before you're ready; be kind to yourself. Moving on doesn't require starting a new relationship as soon as you end one. Beginning something new means moving past the past and finding healing. Ending a relationship may bring significant suffering and loss, and resisting the need to grieve might produce further issues in the future. Never use harmful or risky methods to vent powerful emotions, such as wrath. Try writing a letter to your ex and then burning it. You may also attempt running or boxing as activities. Permit yourself to confront your intense feelings in a private setting, such as a diary, a close friend, or a therapist.

Remove Painful Memories

Let go of things that connect you to that past. After a breakup, there are always things and places that remind us of our ex; this can cause us to idolize the *'good old days'* when things were much better than the present.

If you enjoy preserving mementos of the past out of sentimental value, it would be a good idea to store them in a box at the back of your cabinet until you are ready to reflect on the past again.

Look For the Lessons

Think about what you can learn from the event as you reflect on it. Accept responsibility for your role in the relationship's demise and utilize it as a platform for personal growth. Perhaps you struggle with jealousy or want to practice setting limits.

Don't dwell on what you may have or ought to have done. You may find it difficult to move ahead and accept what has happened if you think about something repeatedly and compulsively. Be truthful with yourself about your areas of potential growth and what you would want to focus on for your next relationship.

Work On Yourself

Think about your requirements. You already possess all you require for balance and wholehearted living. Feelings, murmurs, and ideas you can't shake will reveal the clues.

Pay attention to these feelings and ideas. Your gut instinct is in tune with what you require. Don't ignore it, bury it further inside of you, or turn it off. This is your chance to show yourself the love you deserve if you've experienced a lot of neglect in your life.

Focus on What's Important

Reflecting on what you want from your future relationship doesn't need to be complicated. Make a list of your priorities and areas where you will not tolerate compromise. For instance, it's possible that your ex had trouble communicating or didn't try to get to know your pals.

You may want to put these things on your list of future red flags. Avoid wrongly assessing people based on slight similarities to your ex or comparing everyone to your ex.

Don't Focus on Your Past

You no longer need to be wounded by your wounds. They may now put in a lot of effort for you since they see the evidence of your tenacity, courage, and strength. You'll need to illuminate them first. You won't be able to notice them approaching when they collide with you if you keep them in the dark.

Let It Go

Forgiveness or letting go does not imply forgetting or ignoring the wrong that was done to you. Moreover, it need not entail reconciliation with the wrongdoer. You can focus on yourself and move on with your life more easily when you are forgiven.

You might never get over the person or thing that hurt or insulted you. But, you may loosen your grasp on that act by practicing forgiveness. It may assist in releasing you from the grip of the wrongdoer.

In certain cases, forgiving someone might even elicit sentiments of compassion, empathy, and understanding for the person who injured you. It is possible to experience better health and mental tranquility by letting go of past wrongs and resentment.

The ability to forgive can lead to;

Healthier Relationships

Instead of dwelling on what someone might have said to you, you are free to concentrate on the various connections in your life. If you took offense at something they might have said or done, communicate with them and let them know.

Improved Mental Health

You can move on from the situation and stop worrying about it all the time. As a result, there is less anger toward the other person and less despair, worry, and stress.

Also, it directly impacts your physical well-being by decreasing blood pressure, sustaining a stronger immune system, enhancing heart health, and boosting self-esteem.

Letting the Past Go

Moving on may be a challenging and painful process. Just like everything else, getting over a loss, whether a breakup or leaving a job, won't endure indefinitely.

It might be difficult to tell if you're genuinely over something, but fortunately, there are signals that you have moved on.

You stop living mindlessly

You start from the point of intention and worth rather than doing things to divert, numb, or remain busy. What do you need and feel like doing becomes important. You put your wants ahead of your negative emotions.

You have control over your emotions

You can control strong emotions like rage, hurt, and sadness. You may quickly glance at the feelings you buried that make you think of your ex or past. But you do not experience emotional overload when reflecting on your history.

You release tension & trauma

You're more receptive to physical contact from others, such as hugs or embraces. After rethinking the incident, you do not have headaches, migraines, or a sense of sadness.

You do not isolate yourself

You gradually let more individuals into your intimate emotional circle. You start expressing your demands and requirements. Maybe you expose more hidden aspects of yourself to others.

You let people see you crying, feeling powerless, unhappy, and annoyed. You start to replace your ingrained sense of independence with dependency, community, and connection.

You reflect on life

You start to become aware of your stresses, vulnerabilities, and triggers. You learn to distinguish between danger, safety, and trust while living in the present.

You want learn from the past

Looking at your past is the greatest way to understand who you are. When you start anything new, you won't make the same mistakes you made in the past since you've learned from your experiences. When you advance in life, you comprehend and refer to your prior experiences. You modify and adapt things in ways that are beneficial for you rather than continuing your old habit.

Life is an ongoing story.

We are always learning and growing as individuals. Getting stuck in the past is like sitting at the bus station and watching the buses go by one by one. You miss every opportunity to move closer to the destination. In life, not a single day would go by without you ever learning anything from it.

However, if you are stuck at the bus stop, you cannot learn new things. So, try to get up and hop on the next bus. You might not know where it is headed, but as long as you don't remain stuck at the station, you will reach somewhere.

CHAPTER. 24

Benefits of Sex and Communication in a Relationship

"Sex is not marriage but sex is part of marriage."

– Justice Kojo Betil

Given how frequently it is addressed in pop culture, online relationship columns, and over drinks with close friends, it's no surprise that you'll often find yourself wondering, how important is sex in a relationship?

This question could seem even more pressing if you are in a relationship where the sex isn't quite where you or your partner want it to be. Or perhaps you're simply interested in it since you like having sex or find it quite dull.

The significance of sex in a relationship can vary depending on the individual.

Increasing sex in a supportive relationship has a lot of advantages. Positive improvements like lowered blood pressure, less stress, more closeness, and even a decreased divorce rate are associated with higher rates of sexual engagement. Sex isn't the most crucial aspect of a relationship, but it is a crucial component of building a happy and healthy relationship, even if it may not always appear as a requirement for a relationship to succeed.

Some of the reasons why and how sex helps your relationship include the following:

Feeling Closer to Your Partner

Oxytocin levels are further raised, in both men and women, by sexual activity, which fosters a greater connection between the two. Oxytocin, a hormone associated with emotions of love and connection that can enhance physical pleasure during sexual activities, not only makes you feel closer to your spouse but also helps builds faithfulness by dissuading you from becoming close to other possible partners.

Showing Affection to Your Partner

When you have sex, you can convey how you feel about one another through your actions in the most intimate manner. You may express your love and your confidence in them. Showing affection through sexual pleasure can also deepen your relationship and help you connect with your partner.

Finding Sex Fun and Pleasurable

Your body offers you a natural high during an orgasm. This releases endorphins, chemicals that prevent pain and improve your mood, giving you a happier, calmer, and more relaxed feeling, resulting in a desire to continue having sex.

Feeling Confident and Sexy

Sexual activity can help you gain self-confidence and adopt a healthier, more optimistic attitude about yourself and your body image. Studies also show that regular sexual activity may contribute to a person's overall health. An increase in affection, trust, and love between two lovers is frequently associated with having sex.

Psychological Benefits of Sex

Making love has several emotional and psychological advantages. Sex has been directly related to a higher quality of life in several studies. Among these advantages are the following;

A Better Self-Image

Sex may increase self-esteem and decrease insecurity, which results in more favorable impressions of oneself. It gives one a happier body image as compared to what they're used to seeing every day on social media platforms and other mediums. Being seen as desirable, regardless of body type can make one feel better about themselves and let go of any hang-ups caused by societal beauty perceptions.

Higher Rates of Happiness

A 2015 Chinese study found that having more consensual and higher-quality sex makes people happier.

More Bonding

Endorphins, one class of chemicals that lessen irritation and depressive symptoms, are among the chemicals generated during sex and released in the brain. Oxytocin contributes to feelings of serenity and fulfillment. Also, as I just explained, it encourages you to stick with your relationship.

Stress Relief

You may unwind and distract yourself from daily concerns and anxiety by having sex. While our body releases endorphins and oxytocin during sex, these feel-good chemicals foster emotions of connection and relaxation while also assisting in the prevention of anxiety and sadness. With benefits that extend far into the next day, sexual activity also lowers stress response chemicals, including cortisol and adrenaline (epinephrine).

Quality Sleep

The hormone prolactin, which promotes sleep, is released during orgasms. This makes sleep quality better and leads to more restful sleep.

Physical Benefits of Increased Sex

Although it should be quite obvious how sex enhances emotional wellness, there are also some physical advantages to having sex.

A few of these are;

Better Physical Fitness

Sex is also considered a form of exercise. In fact, according to the American Heart Association, sexual engagement is similar to doing moderate cardio exercises, such as brisk walking or ascending flights of stairs. Your abdominal and pelvic muscles might become more toned and tightened during sex. Additionally, improved muscle tone helps women have better bladder control.

Enhanced Brain Function

According to preliminary research on rats, more frequent sex was associated with greater cognitive performance and the development of new brain cells. Since then, investigations on humans have revealed similar advantages.

In a 2018 study including over 6,000 people, regular sex was associated with superior memory function in people over the age of 50.

Improved Immune Function

More sexual activity is beneficial for immune system health. Frequent sex may even reduce your risk of contracting the flu or a cold.

Lower Pain Levels

Sexual endorphins contribute to more than only peaceful and calm feelings of well-being. These sex endorphins help the nervous system and tend to lessen back and migraine discomfort.

Weight Loss

You can burn as many as 200 calories during 30 minutes of sexual activity. Additionally, the hormones released during sex can help reduce unnecessary cravings for food.

Positive Cardiac Effects

Lower systolic blood pressure has been associated with penetrative sexual activity, but not with masturbation. It was found that elevated blood pressure increases the risk of heart disease and stroke. However, the healthy cardiac workout you get through sexual activity tends to widen blood arteries, lower blood pressure, and increase oxygen flow throughout the body.

Additional Physical Benefits

Increased sexual activity enhances desire and vaginal lubrication. What's surprising is that regular sexual activity is linked to shorter menstrual cycles and less uncomfortable cramps. In addition, the release of the hormone DHEA by the body during orgasm may give one an enhanced sense of smell, better teeth, better digestion, and radiant skin.

Primal Sex

The best sex doesn't start in our heads. Instead, we must let our more instinctual, animalistic parts take the initiative. Everyone wants their spouse to have this energy, which comes more easily in new relationships when the neurochemicals of desire are at their highest levels.

Nevertheless, unadulterated passion in a committed relationship might feel too flimsy and dangerous without the help of those delicious neurochemicals. In fact, you haven't found your primordial sexual self if it doesn't feel raw. Occasionally people choose the status quo when I explain to them what passionate sex in a committed relationship actually involves.

Primal sex is a crucial component of a great sex life for the majority of long-term partners. In most cases, you won't find anyone talking about it, but you will have seen depictions of it in popular media like movies, and series and even read about it in romance books where other couples engage in this type of sex.

We can feel some of the emotions through the vicarious experience without taking risks. But suppose you want to have a better sexual relationship with your long-term companion. Here are some broad ideas to get you going;

Embark On it Together

You'll probably feel overly exposed, and your partner could feel intimidated by your heightened vigor. Sex coming from the body might be considerably more intense than sex when you are reacting to your thoughts.

Express Your Body's Desire

It's referred to as embodiment. For most of us, it entails a regular practice of shifting your attention away from your thoughts and onto the bodily sensations you are feeling.

I assure you that this requires effort and practice, such as frequent yoga or meditation. Without trying, we spend much time listening to our thoughts because they are insistent and loud.

Moreover, feeling things involves experiencing emotions like dread or humiliation and physical discomfort. You probably spend more time attempting to separate from your body than you think.

All of us do.

Allow Your Primal Sexual Self to be Your Guide

This is difficult since most of us connect guilt to our primitive sexual drive. We are instructed to keep this aspect of ourselves private. This suggests that our sexual identities are considered embarrassing, even if they facilitate a positive and healthy sexual experience.

It is considered dangerous to reveal this aspect of ourselves. Individuals would sacrifice having fantastic sex merely to avoid the danger of embarrassment.

Learn to Tolerate Sexual Intensities

Enjoy the pure sexual passion of your mates. Any attempt to diffuse it will lessen the likelihood that your spouse will ever reveal that side of themselves to you again.

Sex and Intimacy

Sexual activity and intimacy are sometimes used interchangeably in romantic partnerships. Nonetheless, there is a clear and important distinction between the two.

When problems in relationships emerge, partners frequently rely on one another to recognize the difference between sex and intimacy. Understanding how the two variables can be essential for repairing, maintaining, and enhancing the quality of your relationship.

Intimacy

Although they may and should go hand in hand for real fulfillment, intimacy is something that transcends a physical act.

Real intimacy entails a degree of emotional kinship and trust that deepens the relationship between two people. Each party can be vulnerable in an intimate connection, allowing for a very personal exchange. While a physical connection frequently accompanies this, closeness may also exist without physical contact. There are three forms of intimacy:

Emotional Intimacy

This results from a strong sense of intimacy and trust.

Physical Intimacy

It entails touching in a way that heightens sensations of intimacy and desire.

Sexual Intimacy

This combines emotional intimacy and trust in sexual activities.

All in all, being intimate is being physically near to your companion.

What is Sex to You?

Because sex may mean various things to different individuals, talking about it can be challenging. Yet sex is, in a literal sense, physical. It's the activation of physical desire and the bodily reaction to a stimulus, regardless of the form.

Intimacy is not always necessary for sexual activity. When talking about sex, particularly in a relationship, some people automatically infer closeness. Some may experience sex in an impersonal and distant way. The notion of intimacy does not apply in these situations.

Contrary to popular belief, however, sexual activity frequently involves the formation of sentiments and a physical reaction.

Can You Have One Without the Other?

In short, yes. According to a 2018 study by the National Library of Medicine, long-term love partnerships with higher degrees of closeness are also likely to have higher levels of sexual desire.

You could believe that closeness and sex are connected and cannot exist separately. Nonetheless, they may and frequently do exist separately. After all, relationships can take many different shapes. While casual physical relationships might be founded on sexual accessibility and compatibility, close friendships may include a platonic emotional closeness component.

While closeness and sex may coexist without leading to a better outcome, combining the two strengthens the relationship. Intimacy and diversity of sex are frequently present in loving relationships. To share a life, couples frequently have at least a slight sensation of closeness. This is in favor of some sexual activity. On the other hand, occasional sex partners have a level of trust and connection that makes having sex conceivable.

Sex Can Create an Intimacy Feedback Loop

A National Library of Medicine study published in the Personality and Social Psychology Bulletin in 2017 found a link between frequent sexual activity and general well-being. It also demonstrates how sex fosters love and affection, influencing how frequently people engage in sexual behavior. Thus, having more sex results in having more sex.

Sex uses positive feedback. The term *"positive"* refers to the output intensifying the input, not happiness or goodness. You take action. You enjoy it. You want to do it more. Or, to put it another way, the brain receives signals from the stimulation of the erogenous zones, which records pleasure and encourages you to continue the pleasant action, which results in more pleasure, and so on, until the climax shuts the entire process down.

The feedback loop is straightforward while engaging in sexual activity alone. You do less of what doesn't feel good and more of what does. Yet, having intercourse with another person might result in an imperfectly closed loop, where the knowledge is not effectively sent back to influence the next course of action. That may be a *"noisy"* system, as engineers would say.

The problem is that feedback relies on secondary cues when two (or more) people are engaged. The experience will suffer if the signals coming in are not precise, just as that thermostat set right by the drafty window.

It's generally accepted that some reactions, such as increased blood flow and lubrication, tend to signal sexual desire. Nonetheless, laboratory investigations demonstrate that people occasionally exhibit these reactions even when they are denied, are anxious, or even disgusted. It is also possible to have subjective sexual excitement without a genital reaction. It's interesting to note that contrary to popular belief, women exhibit lesser connections between sex-related emotions and genital reactions.

Most research indicates that the interpretation of physical input varies across the sexes. Context has a stronger impact on women's subjective experiences; *Am I safe? What do I think about this person? Is this proper social behavior?*

This indicates that the feedback loop in women may be louder, have more inputs, and have more opportunities to go awry.

Discussing and talking with your spouse is the simplest way to deal with this. Regardless of how satisfying their sexual encounters may be, some individuals start to feel lonely and alienated if they cannot express a wide variety of feelings with a partner. Making love often brings a feeling of intimacy and emotional connection for many couples.

It takes trust and openness to be in an intimate sexual relationship. Sexual and other types of intimacy, such as emotional and spiritual connection, are related. Foreplay and other types of physical intimacy are also an element of sexual intimacy, which goes beyond intercourse.

Remember that sex involves many types of physical touch and we often look for ways to express love and affection without sex. Frequently, a couple's sexual relationship gets more rewarding the more intimate they become with one another outside of the sexual activity.

Sexual Compatibility

Sexual compatibility is different for different people. Being sexually compatible just means that you and your partner share similar needs, desires, frequency, and preferences regarding sex.

Like everything we have discussed in this book, this doesn't mean that your partner will be a mirror image of your desires and wants. You and your partner will have your own distinct *'wants'* that may tend to overlap with one another.

Sexual compatibility requires time and conscious effort; it does not just happen automatically. Even if you and your spouse have much in common and similar sexual preferences and expectations, you will still have some disparities because these are very personal issues.

Incompatible?

Being aware of the fact that you will occasionally disagree will make you more compatible. You will argue in a good relationship because when you disagree, you understand one another differently. Overcoming disagreement in a healthy manner strengthens your bond. Every relationship has sex-related compatibility concerns. There is no such thing as a perfect match.

That doesn't mean you're incompatible if your sexual requirements don't match; it just indicates you're normal. Don't let your disagreements deter you from talking about what you want; instead, frame them as requests rather than complaints. It will go a lot further to say, *"Your hands feel dry, let's do something about it!"* than to say, *"I don't enjoy your touch because your hands feel gross."*

Quality Over Quantity

It's natural to consider how frequently you engage in sexual activity while considering your compatibility. Yet this is just one element of compatibility. You'll be able to concentrate on overcoming your disparities in desire levels once you start concentrating on the quality of your sexual relationships.

When one person craves sex more than the other, many worry that this will make them incompatible. This imbalance is inevitable, but if you can change your attention from frequency to what you're doing to preserve and strengthen your sexual connection, it will be easier to handle.

Don't Be Afraid to Experiment

There are instances when you may not have yet discovered what turns you on and makes your sexual experience amazing. You shouldn't be hesitant to experiment because of this.

Perhaps you can explore sex toys, such as a bullet vibrator for clitoral stimulation, kinky clothes, or role-playing. This may seem excessive or kinky, but occasionally you need to go a bit kinky to clear your mind. Just respect your and your partner's boundaries, but have the intention of it being a fun experience.

Vulnerability Isn't Always a Good Thing

Being vulnerable has its drawbacks, particularly in the context of personal relationships. Vulnerability is indeed necessary for a successful relationship, but it would be challenging to build trust with someone who just replies to your probing inquiries and remarks with "good" or "oh, that stinks."

To be able to open up, you must be able to talk about your fears, your dreams, the pain that is holding you back, what you believe to be your purpose in life, why it bothers you when your partner eats more of your fries than they should after claiming not to be hungry, and a long list of other topics. You must be able to put your whole faith in the other person. The advantages of doing this are obvious: You develop a closer bond with your spouse, one that sets them apart from even your closest friends.

In some cases, vulnerability can have disadvantages, though. You give up some of your control by becoming vulnerable, which is where trust in your relationship is important.

What if your spouse does something that makes you feel uncomfortable? Maybe they are acting strangely when they reply to your texts, or maybe they were just acting differently in the last chat you had with them before you left. They could even ask you to have morning sex or engage in another sort of sexual activity that you may not enjoy. Unless you're a robot, that will—to some extent—have an impact on you and the rest of your day. You'll consider it frequently and occasionally experience deep-seated uneasiness.

Stoicism won't be able to stop that. Even if you break up with your spouse, if they do anything that makes you feel humiliated or disgusted, it will affect you for much longer than a day. It seems strange to realize that something entirely beyond your control—the deeds of someone else—can have such a tremendous impact on you, whether you want it to or not and whether you deserve it or not.

Keep in mind that some level of vulnerability is acceptable, like letting your partner try new things in bed, having them experiment, introducing something new in the relationship, etc. But, always being vulnerable and letting your partner do what they want can create a negative feedback loop.

Your partner would, intentionally or unintentionally, make you vulnerable, and while it may be alright to give in sometimes, if you do not like something, do not indulge in it. Constantly letting your partner do as they please will only affect your self-esteem, making your partner think you are fine with anything. The simplest solution to this is communication.

Communicate with your partner and let them know what you want. As I have said in a previous chapter, be aware of your sexual boundaries and do not let anyone cross them. Maintaining your sexual boundaries and respecting your partner's boundaries help both of you to feel comfortable around each other.

Talking About Sex is a Skill

Our lives are influenced by the implications of sex and sexuality, from actions to advertising. Nevertheless, having sex-specific terminology doesn't necessarily translate into easy discussions. This is particularly true when verbalizing what we desire from sex, even while engaging. Successful sex involves communication. One essential skill is the ability to discuss the type of sex we have or desire to have. You already know that discussing sex in your relationship is appropriate. It's the advice you always see in the conclusion of every article you read when you're up late at night researching your most private and embarrassing difficulties.

Your sexual desires are radically out of sync?

Have a discussion on it!

You have been in a protracted dry period; when was your last sexual encounter?

Talk about it.

Do you want your lover to quit acting in a way you secretly despise in the bedroom?

Well, you guessed it—discuss it.

I cannot stress how important it is to talk to your partner about your feelings. You or your partner may feel weird at first, but gradually, as you explain to them why you are doing this, they will understand and start communicating with you. The story of your life can only be told if you tell it. Your partner can't read your mind, and neither can you read your partner's mind. So, just name your intentions and start tenderly with the conversation, not confrontationally.

Letting your partner know what you want and knowing what they want in return will strengthen the relationship in the long run.

The Great Egoic Cape—Learn When to Make it Invisible

Everybody has an ego which is often an integral part of our personality. People can often use both terms interchangeably, although personality and ego are not the same. The ego is only one aspect of a person's whole personality.

The reality principle, on which the ego is based, aspires to find realistically and socially acceptable means to satisfy our wants and desires. When choosing to act on or ignore our impulses, the reality principle assesses the advantages and disadvantages of a particular course of action.

The informal term "ego" is frequently used to imply that someone has an exaggerated sense of self and is looked upon negatively because of this perception. But, the ego also has a beneficial effect. It keeps you grounded in reality and prevents your desires and self-righteous judgments from pushing you too far toward your most primal urges or moralistic ideals.

Strong self-awareness is a sign of a healthy ego.

Sigmund Freud, one of the most fascinating and prominent figures in the field of psychology, compared the ego to a person and our ambitions and needs to a horse that the person is riding.

While the rider gives direction and control, the horse delivers force and motion. But without the rider, the horse would roam aimlessly, doing anything it desires without holding back. The rider (the ego) is the one who commands the horse (our ambitions and needs) and gives it direction.

Secondary process thinking, in which the ego looks for something in the real world that resembles the mental image generated by our needs and desires, is another method by which the ego releases tension brought on by unfulfilled impulses. Here, the ego starts to behave negatively rather than being beneficial.

Ego – The Positive and Negative

When I talk about positive and negative egos, I am mainly referring to the outcome and how it affects our personalities. Happiness comes from having a positive ego. We feel serenity, inner peace, and contentment when we keep a positive outlook, even when everything seems to be working against us.

This is because having a healthy ego allows us to monitor our wants and needs. For instance, imagine you are in a meeting, and you feel hungry all of a sudden. Your first response would be to get something to eat. However, your ego will stop you from doing that, as that would be inappropriate and rude. This is an example of a positive ego.

A negative ego, on the other hand, mostly causes suffering, anguish, discontent, and unease. Most decisions in this situation are made impulsively, which never gives your spirit a chance to emerge. This also causes internal sensitivity in situations that could affect one's sense of self-worth.

For instance, what if you realize that you're in the wrong during an argument with someone, a friend, family, an acquaintance, or even your partner? The natural feeling from a situation like this would be guilt and shame, making you want to apologize or acknowledge that you are wrong.

However, to hide this feeling, your ego steps in and makes you overlook your mistakes, finding reasons to justify your claim. Even if you see that the situation is getting worse, your ego will focus more on being right than wanting to admit that you're wrong, preventing you from seeing the bigger picture, where accepting that you're wrong might help you grow.

It is important to note that not all results you get from a positive ego will be positive and vice versa. That is why it is important to listen to your ego and what your spirit and soul have to offer. Only letting your ego speak will give you a myopic view where you cannot see the bigger picture. Your ego cares only for you, ignoring the needs and wants of others around you.

Ego and Relationships

A big ego is a kryptonite to a happy romantic relationship. It tends to cause conflict between you and your partner. When making choices about love, we allow our egos to get the upper hand. This is an issue since the ego, when given the lead, is incapable of forming relationships. Instead, the ego seeks to control to receive love.

Excessive ego could lead to a toxic relationship. Your ego is the part of you that fights for your *'interests,'* not caring about what happens to others around you. This means that when your interests clash with those of others, your ego takes over.

You'll likely detect your egotism starting to creep in during confrontational arguments or when you feel threatened.

When the Ego is at Work

If you are aware of when the problem is affecting your relationship, you can take action by adopting ego-taming methods, which can help you to strengthen or rebuild your relationship.

Constant Judgment, Criticism, Put-Downs, and Ridicule

It may be a sign of narcissism if you or your partner acts as though they are the center of the universe. A narcissist has little regard for the feelings of others, especially in their relationship.

To convince people to cooperate and accomplish what they want, they tend to manipulate them. Some narcissistic behaviors include boasting about how superior one is to others and talking about oneself all the time.

Since they are so preoccupied with themselves, they also frequently fail to interpret social cues. In most cases, relationship problems are brought on by narcissism because they treat their partner with such toxicity.

After a while, they won't even attempt to compromise since they will feel there is no room for it.

Not Owning Up and Being Proud

Selfishness and pride can cause relationship problems that start small but eventually snowball out of proportion and ruin a connection. When an egocentric partner believes they are better than their mate, pride and arrogance result. A relationship becomes unhealthy and unbalanced when one spouse always seems to have the upper hand, and there is no healthy balance between the power dynamics of the couple. An egocentric individual tends to act in a superior manner, is condescending, and does everything they can to hide their mistakes so no one else can see them.

Even after being discovered, they will still keep trying to hide the truth and distort the facts instead of dealing with the actual problem.

I'm Always Right

Everyone wants to be right occasionally, but this desire shouldn't be constant, nor is it always possible for someone to always be right. A person who must always be correct tends to disregard their partner's sentiments. They are only interested in getting their way and persuading others to concur with them. They're also very defensive, not wanting to hear another viewpoint and barely ever listening to the other individual.

They'll put everything else aside to be in the right and keep pushing until the other partner caves. Most of us tend to believe that it's time for a new relationship when these things occur. However, in such scenarios, we need to learn to control our egos and not stoop to their level. It can be difficult to keep your ego in check, but if you are successful at it, your feeling of self-worth may grow. The ability to properly deal with your triggers is a tremendous accomplishment.

Keeping Your Ego in Check

Keeping your ego in control can be challenging. Here are some strategies to help you do just that.

Set Higher Goals

If you have not accomplished what you aim for, you might find it difficult to keep your ego in check and stop it from turning on you. Instead of doubting yourself and letting your negative ego consume you, work toward having smaller, achievable goals. Continue to improve your knowledge, connections, and the quality of your life. Years from now, you will thank yourself when you see how far you have come.

Focus on living your life and communicating with your loved ones. There is always room for growth and learning, or perhaps you have a talent that would be useful to others. Even the wealthiest people on the planet constantly strive to go above and beyond, both literally and metaphorically.

Success Doesn't Last

Everybody has moments of complacency in their lives. Instead of moving forward, we start sliding back or staying in one place. This isn't always terrible, but it could harm us and our mental health.

The unpleasant reality is that success is not enduring.

But, while our accomplishments make us feel good about ourselves, keep in mind that there is still a lot of work to be done. Build a legacy of tangible accomplishments that lasts longer than fleeting success.

Value and Build True Friendships

Everyone wants to be liked and accepted. Making friends may keep us grounded and headed in the correct direction. When our relationships go beyond the superficial, our friends can support us in managing our egos and serve as a reminder when it starts to spiral out of control.

Recognize Your Ego

Every move you make will be questioned by your ego. It adopts a frightened voice making you doubtful and conveys anxiety and uncertainty. If you ever try to act in accordance with your intuition, and a small voice questions your decision, that's usually your ego making you second guess yourself.

It's the part of you that, while you're trying to lose weight, urges you to eat junk food because you 'deserve' it, then it turns around and berates you for doing so. Once you know this, you can catch your ego and subdue it if you learn what it sounds like.

The Ego Accomplishes Nothing

Anyone's recipe for success must include a strong desire to succeed. Your highest objective can only be achieved if you fully commit to pursuing it with everything you have. Nevertheless, when you devote so much to a single objective, it's simpler for your ego to undermine your self-assurance.

Being ego-driven isn't always damaging if it draws inspiration from the proper places. Yet, the outer environment cannot give birth to your objectives; they must be internal. We struggle to get past our setbacks largely because of them.

We have the tendency to judge ourselves too much based on what other people think of us. You'll constantly live with a sense of insecurity if you gauge your value by how you compare to others. What's best is to know your skills and own them. There will always be someone better than you but there's only one you.

Communicating from your ego is limited in its effectiveness. Remember that your ego is a part of you and that acting and listening only through it will confine you to your own small universe.

Your Ego

As I said, our ego is a part of us and our personality. It plays a big part in who we are, and abandoning it or sidelining it is something that is not possible. Sure, we can tone it down to some extent, but we cannot eradicate it. Our egos help us accomplish difficult tasks, play a part in building our self-worth, and also help us refrain from our intrusive thoughts.

In more ways than one, our ego and the drive to constantly prove ourselves as better than others is what propels our constant evolution. However, if it were not for that and the curiosity of humans, why would we even step out to explore the world?

It's because we want to prove that we are *'better.'* Giving you a reason to leap forward is how our ego benefits us. So, our egos do serve a purpose. However, don't let your ego run wild. While our egos did take us to the moon, it was only by limiting it that are able to live with other humans in a society.

It is important to put a break on it every once in a while, and make sure that you are not stepping out of bounds. Our egos are like fires. They show us the way in the dark, but can also burn us and everything around us if not controlled.

Don't Get All Personal About It

The first thing that you have to learn is that everyone makes mistakes. If you get personal about every little thing that your partner does, it will lead to fights and arguments. As I have said countless times throughout this book, you and your partner are different people. Having disagreements is healthy and something that will always happen. If your partner isn't willing to disagree with you or doesn't really talk with you, then it is time to reevaluate things.

Accept All Your Mistakes

Don't be stubborn; accept it if you make a mistake. It will be hard at first, so instead of outright saying that you were wrong, stay silent during the argument, or refrain from adding fuel to the fire.

Once your partner has calmed down, tell them it was your fault. If you are the aggressor, then stop and break off the argument. Take a walk, calm down, and then admit to your mistake. Don't just admit to it; find a workable solution to your problems.

Over time, after a month or two of this, you will see that you can control yourself and accept your mistakes, and your partner will also start respecting you.

Stop Being Afraid of Looking Silly

It is all right to let your thoughts run wild sometimes. Try doing something you think is silly and dumb; defeat your ego by not letting it have its way. This will also improve your self-confidence as you can step out of the box and do what you want without caring about what others think.

Our spiritual selves and energy have a lot to do with controlling the flow of our egos. As I said at the beginning of this chapter, our ego is a part of our personality, and our relationship with it will affect our personality.

Once you figure this part out, you will learn to accept your ego and let go of the negative things. Your ego may be helpful to you, but imposing it on others, especially your partner, can have consequences. There is no '*I*' in a relationship but a '*we*' that is built from compromise, restraint, and acceptance.

"EGO is the only requirement to destroy any relationship, so be the bigger person and let go of the E and let it GO."

—Christine Benjamin

CHAPTER.26

Outcomes of Accepting Yourself from Within

We all want to be accepted, no matter where we come from or how we interact with the people around us. To be loved and accepted by the people who surround us is innate. However, in the pursuit of getting others to accept and love us, we forget to give love to ourselves.

We neglect our needs and focus on the latest fashion trends, hoping we would be able to 'fit in' to society. Unfortunately, instead of solving the problem, it drives us to push away our natural and true selves in favor of what others want from us.

For someone to accept and value you, you need to start accepting and valuing yourself.

Self-Love

Self-love is a feeling of admiration for oneself that develops from deeds that promote our mental, emotional, and spiritual development. Having high regard for your own pleasure and well-being is what it means to love oneself. It entails attending to your own needs and not putting your well-being at risk to appease others. You must never accept anything less than what you deserve. You might be limited in every aspect of your life if you lack self-love.

You may not be able to realize your full potential since its lack will undermine your confidence. High self-acceptance individuals are more tolerant of criticism. They are aware that it's okay to accept oneself while striving for ongoing progress.

Self-love includes your ideas and feelings about yourself in addition to how you treat yourself. It is about the things you would do for yourself, how you would speak to yourself, and how you would feel about yourself in a way that expresses love and concern when you conceive self-love.

You generally form a favorable opinion of yourself when you love yourself. This does not imply that you constantly feel good about yourself. It is not practical. For instance, even when feeling sad, furious, or disappointed with oneself, a person might still love oneself. Consider how this operates in other partnerships if it's unclear.

Even if you occasionally experience resentment or disappointment toward your child, you may still love them. Your affection for them guides how you interact with them, even when you're upset and disappointed. You can forgive them, consider their needs, satisfy them, and make judgments that are in their best interests because of that love.

Self-love is pretty similar to that.

This implies that if you understand how to love others, you also understand how to love yourself. This is a crucial component of the equation because if you only love yourself, you could become narcissistic.

Self-Love vs. Narcissism

Psychologists and therapists do not advocate elevating oneself above others when they advocate for self-love. Narcissists typically think they're superior to other people and refuse to accept blame for their shortcomings. Also, they look for excessive amounts of approval and attention from others.

Narcissists are also non-empathetic. Since we do not exist in solitude, we cannot learn to love ourselves in that manner. Being human means requiring other people for support and care. The degree of love we have experienced from others frequently determines our ability to love ourselves. But in reality, we can only love others to the depth that we love ourselves.

It's great to shout "love yourself" at the top of our lungs, but for those who find it difficult, who have had their needs ignored, who had a number of unsatisfying relationships, extended periods of loneliness or isolation, abusive partners, or emotionally absent parents, it can leave them feeling inadequate or like there is something wrong with them. These people often exclusively show affection to themselves and find "comfort" in themselves.

On the other side, self-love doesn't involve bragging about how amazing you are. Healthy self-lovers embrace and care for themselves despite their flaws and failures because they are aware of how flawed and fallible they are. You can still be humble and have self-love. It simply means you may treat yourself with the same care you show to others; it does not exclude you from caring about others.

Self-Love vs. Self-Acceptance

These two ideas are not the same, even if they are linked. Self-acceptance is a general affirmation of who you are, whereas self-love is the value or worth you place on yourself.

The key to self-acceptance is accepting both our positive and bad sides. This translates to an absolute acceptance of oneself. Accepting oneself completely by acknowledging and embracing your flaws or faults.

Self-acceptance is the capacity to view oneself objectively, without bias, and to be "fine" with oneself. You may accept every aspect of who you are, including your flaws and successes, anxieties, environment, physical appearance, and values, without conditions. Whether you like them or not, they are the realities about you and are an important part of your flawed human life. You already deserve and are entitled to love, care, success, health, and well-being simply for being a human; nothing about you has to change. Self-acceptance also includes behaviors like accepting your humiliating moments, attributing them to being human, and letting them go.

Self-love, on the other hand, entails taking care of, and kindly supporting oneself. You must identify the aspects of yourself you are not ready to embrace if you want to learn to love yourself. Accepting every aspect of who you are is essential to loving yourself. You can only do this once you stop criticizing yourself.

According to research, the instant we stop being so critical of ourselves, our self-esteem increases. Self-love encompasses self-care as well! After all, loving someone involves more than simply feeling; it also involves "doing."

Regardless of how they define it, people with a strong sense of self-love frequently desire and actively seek improved health and well-being. They devote time and money to caring for themselves, doing things they like, eating well, and having satisfying relationships. Since they rank just as high on their priority list as the people they care about, persons with great self-love may experience little to no guilt when they take care of themselves. They recognize that they are deserving of the same treatment they provide to others.

Doing things for oneself and others while maintaining a positive self-image is frequently possible.

Importance of Self-Love

The best investment you can make in yourself is strengthening your connection with yourself. According to studies, when you love and care for yourself, you experience more happiness and a lower chance of depression.

Achievements, satisfaction, and difficult circumstances are like a disease that challenges your resilience and tests how strong your self-esteem really is. At the same time, low self-esteem can fuel high-risk behaviors, including drug misuse, depression, anxiety, and other mental health issues. It encourages you to engage in harmful behaviors in an effort to plug the gaping hole that only genuine self-love can close.

Reduces Stress

Self-love includes taking care of oneself. When you value who you are, you can spot the warning symptoms of burnout and take action to lessen your stress. You might not feel that you deserve a break if you lack self-love.

Accepting the idea of doing something "just for me" may be quite difficult. As a result, you are more inclined to persevere during a trying moment. While under stress, those who have healthy self-love are more apt to take the time to look after themselves.

Allows You to Manage Anxiety and Depression Symptoms

According to research, those who practice self-compassion frequently are less likely to experience anxiety or despair. This doesn't imply that being nervous or unhappy prevents you from liking yourself. Self-love components like self-care, self-compassion, and encouraging self-talk might aid with symptom management is implied. The frequent misconception that having a mental illness is somehow your responsibility may be liberated with self-love.

Improves Emotional Resilience

It's easy to fall into hopelessness when things are tough. Depending on the situation, you could have to deal with those who hold you responsible for your problems. In such a case, you could begin to hold yourself accountable.

Self-love puts things in perspective and counters negative, critical self-talk. Self-love enables you to go on and learn from your mistakes, even if they led to your troubles. This strengthens your emotional fortitude and gets you ready for difficulties down the road.

Increases Your Happiness

Self-acceptance and self-love are associated with greater life satisfaction and, thus, greater pleasure. It's difficult to be joyful about anything when you're always examining your shortcomings and evaluating your decisions.

Self-acceptance enables you to admit that despite your imperfections, you are still deserving of acceptance and encouragement. It enables you to accept yourself the way you are. Your flaws become stepping stones through which you allow yourself to improve your character and become a better person. You're more likely to consider yourself a close buddy if you adore yourself.

Boosts Your Confidence

If you're continuously criticizing yourself, it's quite challenging to feel confident. Low self-esteem is a common challenge for those who have negative self-talk. Naturally, a loss of confidence follows.

Self-love is a terrific way to train your confidence to feel more self-assured. You'll feel your confidence escalating if you acknowledge your value and abilities and practice compassion when you're angry with yourself.

Improves Relationships

There's a phrase that goes, *"Until you love yourself, you can't fully love others."*

Although a bit excessive, loving oneself may enhance your interactions with others. You won't feel as reliant on other people for your feeling of value when you love yourself. This makes it easier for you to establish boundaries or, if necessary, leave toxic relationships. As they have a greater understanding of who they are, people who love themselves can also better recognize the kind of relationships they desire and don't want.

Increases Productivity

The productivity killer is procrastination. You could use severe methods to motivate yourself. Threats of self-punishment are a tactic used by some people to try to start an activity, but research indicates that it is ineffective as a motivator. It's best to be kind to yourself when you put things off. Make the most of your "failure" as a teaching moment for the future. You'll feel lighter and more prepared to make behavioral adjustments as opposed to being weighed down by self-criticism.

Helps in Developing Healthier Habits

According to data, choosing to love yourself might influence your health decisions. Researchers discovered that people were more motivated to make positive changes in their lives when they accepted themselves without passing judgment in a meta-analysis of 15 studies in the field of health psychology.

This was the situation, according to research, when people started to stop smoking. Exercise and eating more healthfully were other actions. Those who practiced self-compassion developed new, healthier habits.

Physical Benefits

Prioritizing your needs, including your body's need for movement and stretching, is a sign of self-love. Making time for the gym or a stroll in the park might help you feel less anxious in the short term and enhance your thinking, learning, and decision-making skills.

Over time, regular exercise improves brain health, helps you control your weight, and lowers your chance of developing certain cancers and other ailments. Because what you put inside your body may impact how you feel and respond to uncomfortable situations, taking care of yourself involves what you eat. Also, as you learn to love yourself, you stop punishing yourself for every calorie you consume and start allowing yourself to indulge in your favorite foods.

Helps in Achieving Your Goals

Self-love teaches that your goals should come first. Going for what you want in life is not being egotistical, especially if it will benefit you. Others may attempt to convince you otherwise, but you should live your life in a way that makes you happy as long as you aren't stepping on other people in order to achieve your objectives.

Also, self-love gives you the resources to realize your ambitions, such as lowered stress levels, emotional fortitude, greater output, and confidence. Together, these things support your progress in life and bring you one step nearer to your ultimate objective.

Loving Yourself Helps You Love Others

We frequently devote a lot of time to thinking about ourselves. How we behave in public, how we appear, how to have a good romantic life, or how to advance in our careers. Some of us might even spend a lot of time contemplating ways to quit thinking too much, pondering how to get mentally calm, and quit worrying about the future.

While occasionally going inward might be helpful, doing so excessively causes us to spend less time and energy on others. To put it another way, you may concentrate more on others around you when you pay less attention to yourself.

If you first extend it to yourself, you are more inclined to extend understanding and forgiving love to others. You will decide to value other people's peculiarities more. When anything goes wrong, you don't become overly agitated; instead, you find humor in the situation. You can better appreciate the stage of life you're in when you love yourself. Our ability to trust our instincts and judgment increases when we genuinely respect and love ourselves. It enables us to be brave and sincere.

We start acting more real and living a bigger, kinder, more forgiving version of ourselves. We abandon the limitations we set for ourselves and dare to imagine bigger and wilder dreams. We stop concentrating on the bad things and start noticing the beauty and opportunities both inside and outside of ourselves. We become aware of how wonderful our lives are and throw open the floodgates of appreciation.

We begin to radiate joy, self-assurance, playfulness, calmness, and optimism. To others, it is electric and acts like a strong magnet. The kind of person you're looking for will be drawn to you like a bear emerging from hibernation seeking his first meal.

And when you do, falling in love will be simple. It will be organic. It will flow without restriction or pretense. You'll be inspired and fed by it. Your lives will be even more abundant, joyful, and colorful. You'll look back and wonder why you didn't take the time to fall deeply in love with yourself sooner.

Improves Sexual Health

Accepting oneself and being conscious of one's sexual needs and interests is necessary for sexual wellness. Knowing your body is the first step to loving and embracing it. There are so many contradictory messages around sexuality, which can cause misunderstanding, social isolation, and destructive thought habits.

One bad event is all it takes to alter our sexual behavior. It's crucial to establish sexual pleasure-centered self-love practices. Building positive relationships with yourself is not promoted. Changing your relationship with yourself can improve your sexual awareness and how you enjoy sex.

Always be open-minded and mindful of your priorities. We live in a world where there are already enough people who despise us for being distinctive. Those people usually have negative thoughts toward us. They may feel just as horrible about themselves as they attempt to make you feel. But, you are aware of all the hardships and effort you have endured. You should be kind to yourself for it and be inspired to begin showing yourself that love right away.